Contemporary
sociology of
the school
General editor
JOHN EGGLESTON

Language, schools
and classrooms

CONTEMPORARY SOCIOLOGY
OF THE SCHOOL

PAUL BELLABY
The sociology of comprehensive schooling

PATRICIA BROADFOOT
Assessment, schools and society

BRIAN DAVIES
Social control and education

SARA DELAMONT
Interaction in the classroom
Second edition

Sex roles and the school

JOHN EGGLESTON
The ecology of the school

RONALD KING
The sociology of school organization

COLIN LACEY
The socialization of teachers

PETER MUSGRAVE
The moral curriculum

ROY NASH
Schooling in rural societies

PHILIP ROBINSON
Education and poverty

MICHAEL STUBBS
Language, schools and classrooms
Second edition

WILLIAM TYLER
The sociology of educational inequality

TOM WHITESIDE
The sociology of educational innovation

ed. SARA DELAMONT
Readings on interaction in the classroom

eds MICHAEL STUBBS and HILARY HILLIER
Readings on language, schools and classrooms

MICHAEL STUBBS

Language, schools and classrooms

Second edition

METHUEN
London and New York

9750

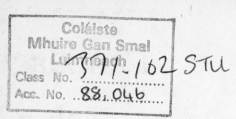
First published in 1976 by
Methuen & Co. Ltd
11 New Fetter Lane, London EC4P 4EE
Reprinted 1978 and 1979
Second edition 1983
Reprinted 1985

Published in the USA by
Methuen & Co.
in association with Methuen, Inc.
733 Third Avenue, New York, NY 10017

Printed in Great Britain
by Richard Clay & Co Ltd
The Chaucer Press
Bungay, Suffolk

British Library
Cataloguing in Publication Data

Stubbs, Michael
  Language, schools and
  classrooms.—2nd ed.—
  (Contemporary sociology of
  the school)
  1. School children—Language
  2. Teachers—Language
  I. Title   II. Series
  371.1′02   LB1027

  ISBN 0-416-35640-0

Library of Congress
Cataloging in Publication Data

Stubbs, Michael, 1947-
  Language, schools and
  classrooms.
  (Contemporary sociology of
  the school)
  Bibliography: p.
  Includes index.
  1. Language arts—Great
  Britain.
  2. Children—Great Britain
  —Language.
  3. Sociolinguistics.
  I. Title.   II. Series.
  LB1576.S87 1983   372.6
  83-7972

  ISBN 0-416-35640-0 (pbk.)

Contents

Editor's introduction   7

Foreword to the second edition   11

1   Why is language important in education?   15
The language of education?   16
Language, learning and classrooms   16
Teacher training and language study   21

2   Some basic sociolinguistic concepts   24
Language and attitudes to language   25
The primitive language myth   30
Standard and nonstandard English   32
Language structure and language use   37
The implication of such distinctions   43

3   Bernstein's theory of restricted and elaborated codes   46
The work of Basil Bernstein   47
Bernstein's early work   49
Bernstein's later work (1973)   56
Do the codes exist?   61
Some possible confusions   63
Conclusions   65

4   Labov and the myth of linguistic deprivation   67
Languages, logic, explicitness and grammar   68
Nonstandard languages as media of education   72
The myth of linguistic deprivation   74
Labov and Bernstein   79
West Indian children in British schools   80
A pseudo-problem?   84

5   The need for studies of classroom language   88
Reasons for studying classroom language   88
Our ignorance of classroom language   90
The rationale for naturalistic studies   94
Teachers as researchers   97

6 Studies of classroom language 99
Commentaries on classroom dialogue 100
The structure of classroom dialogue 107
The classroom as a sociolinguistic setting 111
Studying social processes in classrooms 114

7 Teaching and talking: the hidden
curriculum of classroom talk 118
The hidden curriculum 119
The framing of educational knowledge 121
Discourse structure and assumptions about teaching 124
The social construction of children's ability 128
Teaching as talking: some cross-cultural data 129

8 Towards a sociolinguistic analysis
of language in education 133
Language as evidence for educational statements 134
Language is organized 136
Criteria for studies of language in education 140

9 Some topics for investigation 142

Further reading 149
References and name index 151
Subject index 158

Editor's introduction

Less than a decade ago the 'Contemporary Sociology of the School' series was conceived. Its purpose was to bring together the new and often complex sociological explorations of events in and around the school and its classrooms in a way in which they could be understood and made use of by teachers and other professional workers. An important part of the purpose was also to bring together, with similar clarity, the relevant range of theoretical orientations and research strategies, for without these any new understanding could only be incomplete. The enterprise has been an outstanding success. With the help of an able and enthusiastic team of authors, a group of books has been produced which has been used by tens of thousands of students. The distinctive red volumes have become key texts in their own right in universities and colleges throughout the world.

There is little doubt that the series has made an important contribution to sweeping away many of the misleadingly easy and often unexamined assumptions of the 1960s – such as those about the achievements of working-class children, girls and members of ethnic minorities. The books have illustrated the ways in which individual teachers' and students' definitions of situations can influence events, how perceptions of achievement can not only define achievement itself, but also identify those who achieve; how expectations about schooling can help to determine the nature and evaluations of schools.

The books explore the main areas of the sociology of the school in which new understandings of events are available. Each introduces the reader to the new interpretations, juxtaposes them against the longer-standing perspectives and reappraises the contemporary practices of education and its consequences. Each author in the series has worked extensively in his or her areas of specialism and has been encouraged not only to introduce the reader to the subject but also to develop, where appropriate, his or her own analyses of the issues. Yet though each volume has its distinctive critical approach, the themes and treatments of all of them are closely interrelated. The series as a whole is offered to students who seek understanding of the practice of education in present-day societies, and to those who wish to know how contemporary sociological theory may be applied to the educational issues of these societies.

A new development in the series is the introduction of 'readers' to accompany several of the volumes. These contain a range of papers, many not previously published, which have been selected by the authors of the original volumes to augment and develop their analyses and to help readers to extend their understanding of the fields.

Since the publication of the earlier volumes the pace of research and theoretical development in many of the areas has been rapid – development in which the authors themselves have been actively involved. Nowhere has such development been more rapid than in the study of the language of the school. In this volume Michael Stubbs has revised and rewritten his text which was first published in 1976. He has taken account of remarkable advances in the study of dialect and minority language, the debate on language deficit and the new emphases on the use of language following the publication of major reports in many countries, notably the Bullock Report in Britain. But he also re-emphasizes and sharpens his original concern with the practice of the classroom, showing how the individual teacher can investigate the language of schools and thereby better understand and utilize the regional, social and ethnic diversity they offer. As before the book is characterized by a clarity of presentation that itself constitutes a valuable example of language use.

John Eggleston

Foreword to the second edition

In the seven years since the appearance of the first edition of this book in 1976, a great deal of important work has been published on language in education, and there is probably even greater recognition than seven years ago that a systematic understanding of language is very important to teachers. The major findings and recommendations of the Bullock Report, *A Language for Life* (HMSO, 1975), are still widely cited and influential: a considerable achievement for an official report (see Ch. 1.3).

All the topics which I discussed in the first edition therefore still seem relevant, and I have not omitted anything major in this revised edition. The main changes have been to revise thoroughly and bring up to date all the references and to expand and make more explicit several sections.

Since 1976 many valuable books have made accessible to teachers facts and ideas which are of central importance to education. This work falls into the following main categories.

(1) A great deal of work has been published on the sociology of language in Britain. This includes:

(a) Descriptions of dialects and accents of British English, using modern methods of urban dialectology. For example, Macaulay (1978), Milroy (1980) and Cheshire (1982) provide details of nonstandard dialects in Glasgow, Belfast and Reading respectively, and J. C. Wells (1982), a comprehensive study of English accents. Hughes and Trudgill (1979) summarize some of the main facts and principles.

(b) Descriptions of other dialects of English, in particular Caribbean English: see V. K. Edwards (1979), Sutcliffe (1981), Le Page (1981).

(c) Facts about the distribution of ethnic minority languages in Britain: see Rosen and Burgess (1980). The work of the Linguistic Minorities Project based at the London University Institute of Education is very important and will soon be available in book form.

All of this work provides badly needed information about dialects and languages in Britain.

(2) There has been increased interest in reading and writing as social activities, especially in the ways in which printed and written material are actually used in school classrooms, as opposed to mainly psychological, experimental studies of reading ability: for example, Lunzer and Gardner (1978).

(3) Language disability, in its clinical and pathological aspects, is also an important topic for at least some teachers, although too specialized to be discussed in this book. It is now, for the first time, well provided with introductory and more advanced textbooks which are accessible to teachers: see Crystal (1980) and the associated series edited by Crystal, Studies in Language Disability and Remediation (Edward Arnold).

(4) A large amount of work on classroom language and interaction has continued to be published. Although the descriptions are in some ways more sophisticated, work in this area does not seem essentially different from what was available in 1976. There are, however, excellent studies which relate

12

theory, description and educational practice: a model in this respect is by Willes (in press).

I am particularly aware that this book does not provide any substantial discussion of such major topics as the place of ethnic minority languages in British schools, and the concept of literacy. However, not everything can be covered in a short book, and books which attempt to put across basic concepts in a small space have their own merits. Much relevant material on both these topics is provided in the companion reader to this book, edited by myself and Hilary Hillier (1983), and a discussion of literacy is provided by *Language and Literacy* (Stubbs, 1980).

One very striking development over the past few years is that an increasing number of professional academic linguists have become interested in language in education. For example, two associations of professional linguists, the British Association for Applied Linguistics and the Linguistics Association of Great Britain, contribute to the Committee for Linguistics in Education, which was set up in 1978 and has active programmes of co-operation with teachers. These two organizations are also affiliated to the National Congress on Languages in Education, which was set up in 1976 to study all aspects of foreign language, second language and mother-tongue teaching in Britain, and has already produced many useful reports. It is encouraging that many academic linguists have taken on the responsibility of selecting, interpreting and presenting up-to-date knowledge about language in a way which makes clear its great social and educational importance.

However, it is very disappointing that this flood of excellent academic work has been hindered by the way in which much teacher training has been severely restricted by the closure of courses and whole colleges. In many cases it has been courses in English language and linguistics in education that, as recently established, have been among the first to vanish.

In the preparation of this edition I have received helpful suggestions from Margaret Berry and Patrick J. Finn. I am also most grateful to the teachers and pupils who allowed me to observe and tape-record them and therefore provided many of the ideas discussed here.

Michael Stubbs
Nottingham, 1983

1

Why is language important in education?

There is probably general agreement among educationalists that language is somehow a crucial factor in a child's education. But there is certainly *no* general agreement on precisely *how* 'language' and 'education' are related. How, for example, is language related to learning? How is a child's language related, if at all, to his success or failure at school? Does it make sense to call some children's language 'restricted'? What kind of language do teachers and pupils use in the classroom? Does a child's dialect bear any relation to his or her educational ability? What is the significance of the fact that over a hundred languages are spoken in Britain? Should special educational provision be made for the very high concentrations of speakers of immigrant languages in several areas of the country? These are socially very important questions, because what is at stake is people's beliefs about the place of language in schools and classrooms, and people's tolerance – or lack of it – of regional, social and ethnic variation in language.

This book has two main aims. The relations between language and education are complex, and it is important not to oversimplify them. The first aim is therefore to give readers the necessary concepts for disentangling some of the complexities and for understanding the basic issues in the debate. The second is to suggest some ways in which students and teachers themselves can observe and study how language is used in schools and classrooms.

1.1 The language of education?

(1) See Janet, mother. See Janet play. See John and father.
(2) A: Now, who can tell me what a discjockey is? Brian.
   B: It's on the radio, the man who says what records are going to be played.
   A: Yes, good. On the radio. You get someone who announces the records and says, 'Now for Mrs Smith of 22 High Street, Easthampton' . . .

Even if you did not already know that this book is about language in schools, you would doubtless recognize that these fragments of language were taken from teaching contexts. They are genuine, but stereotypical, examples. (1) is the artificial language unfortunately still found in some reading books for young children: language in a style that no young children (or adults!) would normally use in speech. And (2) is a fragment of tape-recorded classroom dialogue with a teacher asking a question, not because he or she wants to find out something, but to find out if the pupil knows something; and then reformulating the pupil's answer in his or her own words. Schools and classrooms sometimes make strange linguistic demands on pupils.

1.2 Language, learning and classrooms

Imagine going into a dozen different classrooms in different kinds of school. In some classrooms pupils might be doing practical activities, like painting or woodwork, or nonverbal activities, like mathematical calculations. But in most classrooms including maths and woodwork classes, of course, you would find teachers and pupils talking, reading and writing: that is, engaged in *linguistic* activities. Language is a central fact in schools and classrooms, and there are therefore several simple but important reasons why it deserves careful study by anyone concerned with education. Some of these reasons are as follows.

Schools and classrooms are pervasive *language environments*. Pupils are dealing with language for most of the day: with the spoken language of the teacher or of other pupils, and with the written language of books. There is a sense in which, in our culture, teaching *is* talking. Research on traditional, relatively formal, chalk-and-talk classrooms shows that, on average, teachers tend to talk for about 70 per cent of classroom time (Flanders, 1970). If pupils remain in school between the ages of 4 and 16 years they may have over 8000 hours of teacher-talk to listen to! Many cultures have quite different concepts of teaching and learning through practical demonstration, supervised participation, observation and trial and error (see Ch. 7.5). But teaching as we know it is almost inconceivable without language. For us, teaching and learning typically comprise linguistic activities such as: lecturing, explaining, discussing, telling, questioning, answering, listening, repeating, paraphrasing and summarizing. One main aim of this book is therefore to suggest some ways in which such activities can be studied in everyday classroom dialogue.

It is sometimes said that 'every teacher is an English teacher' and that 'every lesson is an English lesson'. By this is meant that a teacher of any subject (not just English, but also maths, geography or chemistry) has to teach the language of his subject. A teacher cannot easily separate teaching facts or concepts in, say, chemistry, from teaching his pupils how to use appropriate terminology, how to construct a coherent argument and how to understand books about chemistry. We do not expect a pupil's essay on chemistry to read like an essay on English literature: not only the subject matter but also the style is quite different. For example, we do not expect a chemistry essay to begin:

Few things can be more beautiful than to watch crystals grow

17

before your eyes in various shapes and hues. Yesterday, my friend and I dropped some warm, strong copper-sulphate solution onto a microscope slide, and watched with delight as the liquid cooled and the tiny crystals took shape.

More appropriate (that is, stylistically conventional) would be:

Two or three drops of warm, concentrated copper-sulphate solution were placed on a microscope slide. As the solution cooled, crystals were deposited. Solutions were selected so that varieties of crystal forms and colours were investigated.

The subject-specific language of an academic subject may have an intellectual function. We are all familiar with the kind of academic specialist (possibly a teacher) who is only happy thinking about his subject in its specialist terminology, and is unable to explain things in everyday language to non-specialists. (Linguists are perhaps particularly guilty of this!) It is often easier to use one technical term to explain another, using terms like counters to be shuffled around, rather than thinking about what they actually mean and relate to in real experience. Conversely, such a teacher may be unable to recognize a valid idea from a pupil if it is not expressed in the style and terminology he is used to. It is not only a matter of specialist jargon – this is usually obvious and everyone is aware of it – it is also a question of the whole style of language considered appropriate for academic discussion (see Ch. 6.1).

Keddie (1971) gives a striking example of how a teacher may pay more attention to a pupil's *style* of language than to the *idea* being expressed. In a science lesson, pupils were shown pictures of a foetus in a womb. One boy asked: 'How does it go to the toilet?' A more conventional formulation might be: How does it dispose of waste products? This is a sensible question, and shows that the pupil is thinking for himself, but the boy could not express himself in this more conventional style, and a teacher later commented that 'he must have been joking'. It is important not to confuse *what* a pupil says with *how* he says it.

I was once castigated by the editor of a book on classroom

research for using too many 'I's' in an article I had sent him. He changed several of my sentences from, for example, 'I will argue that . . .' to 'It will be argued that . . .' At one level, this did not change my meaning, but it changed the overall style.

Some people would argue further that language is somehow related to thinking, learning and cognitive development. The precise relationship between language and thinking is complex and little understood, and has provided philosophical controversy for centuries: Does thought depend on language or vice versa? This formulation of the question is probably too vague to be answerable. But it is at least plausible that higher levels of abstract thinking are supported by language. It is difficult to think about abstract concepts (say, 'exponence' or 'feedback') unless we have convenient labels for them. We are on safer ground, and able to say something more specific by rephrasing the question as: Are there describable linguistic routines through which pupils acquire information and understanding? Phrased in this way, it is possible to study actual classroom dialogue in actual classrooms, and to study how a teacher controls a lesson by opening or closing various learning possibilities to pupils (see Chs 6 and 7). (I will discuss the language–thought problem below only from this relatively restricted point of view, but readers should be aware that many different theories have been proposed by psychologists and philosophers to try and explain how language and thinking are related. A discussion of this large literature is beyond the scope of the present book, but interested readers should consult Greene (1975), who provides a short introduction to the area.)

An often-heard catchphrase in recent years has been that 'educational failure is linguistic failure'. This superficially simple statement covers a highly complex problem, and debate over it has often generated more heat than light. *In some sense*, it is clear that if a school considers a pupil's language to be inadequate, then he or she will probably fail in the formal educational system. But this is a tautology which follows automatically from the pervasive language environment on which schools depend. It merely raises the central question of what linguistic

19

demands schools make on pupils. What does 'linguistically inadequate' mean? Does it mean that the child's language somehow constrains his or her thinking? Or that it causes communication problems with a teacher who may speak a different regional or social dialect? Or that the child cannot read or cannot spell? Or that the child speaks a dialect with low social prestige to which teachers react by calling it 'ugly' or 'slovenly', and in rejecting the child's language reject the child? Clearly, these are all very different kinds of inadequacy. We must beware of oversimplifying the complex relationships between language, social class, educational success and the linguistic demands of everyday life in the classroom.

Changes in academic fashion have variously attributed educational failure to IQ (in the period 1920–40), to home environment (in the 1950s and 1960s), and now (since the 1960s) to language. No *single* factor, however, can explain why some pupils fail where others succeed. Language, social class, home environment and intelligence are all interdependent, and any simple model of language in education will be *over*simple. Certainly, any theory which claims to relate a child's language *directly* to his or her educational success can easily be shown to be inadequate (see Chs 3 and 4). It is the responsibility of teachers and other educationalists, as well as sociologists, to understand the complexities of the debate in this area.

Finally, language is important in education because it is *socially* very important. No dialect is inherently superior or inferior to any other. What we know as standard English (SE) is largely based on the social-class dialect of upper-income groups in south-east England, and is only 'standard' due to historical, geographical and social accidents. (SE is descended from the dialect of educated Londoners which, in the Middle Ages, began to acquire social prestige and to turn from a regional dialect into a social-class dialect. See Ch. 2.3.) But speakers may be at a severe *social* disadvantage if they use nonstandard dialect forms or have nonstandard accents. However groundless such judgements may be, people *are* nevertheless judged intellectually on the basis of minor differences in pronunciation and superficial features of their language. There is *no linguistic* justification for such judgements, but it is an important social fact that A may be thought less intelligent than B because of his regional accent. (It is also reported in the psychological literature that people who wear spectacles are typically assumed to be more intelligent than those who do not!) Such *socio*linguistic phenomena may be crucial in classrooms where teachers and pupils speak different dialects. So it is important that educationalists can distinguish between the characteristics of language itself and the power of people's stereotyped attitudes to language (see Ch. 2.1).

All this might suggest a reformulation of the previous point. Rather than speaking of a pupil's 'linguistic failure', it might be more accurate to speak of sociolinguistic barriers between pupils and the educational system. This point is discussed at length in Chapters 3 and 4.

For these reasons, then – the pervasive language environment of schools; the difficulty of separating conventional styles of language from the content of academic subjects; the complex relationships between language, thinking and educational success; and the power of social attitudes to language – it is important for everyone concerned with schools and classrooms to give language careful study. It is important for very practical reasons that teachers should understand, for example, the nature of people's reactions to different styles and regional varieties of language, and the nature of possible differences between their own language and the language of their pupils. And it is important, too, that students of sociology should understand the complex and often indirect nature of the relationship between language, social class, social groups and education.

1.3 Teacher training and language study

It is because language concerns *all* teachers that the influential Bullock Report makes a strong recommendation that: 'A substantial course of language in education (including reading) should be part of every primary and secondary-school teacher's initial training, whatever the teacher's subject or the age of the children with whom he or she will be working' (HMSO, 1975, p. 515). I strongly endorse this view and intend this book to cover some of what I believe should go into such a course.

There is one interesting, but disturbing, finding in the Bullock Report about the qualifications of teachers. In a survey of 2000 schools in England, the committee found that *almost a third* (32.8 per cent) *of teachers of English had no formal qualifications in English*, that is, no degree, drama qualification, B.Ed. with an English component and so on. Now, of course, formal qualifications may bear little relation to a teacher's actual classroom skill: a teacher with no formal qualifications whatsoever may do excellent work. And it may be that English is often taught by teachers who have had linguistic training through the classics or modern languages. Further, an English degree may not, in any case, be an appropriate qualification for teaching English in a school. Many English degrees contain little language work, and there is no obvious relationship between, say, studying Beowulf and teaching essay writing to 14 year olds! The point is, however, that English is frequently regarded as a subject which can be taught, often part time, by non-specialists who have had little or no linguistic training. No one would regard physics teaching in this amateur way.

Reasons for this neglect of language training for teachers are not hard to find. Different authorities often disagree sharply about what an English teacher should be trying to do. In recent years, justified dissatisfaction with unimaginative teaching of traditional grammar has given way in many places to a 'creative writing' approach. But this approach often leaves teachers wondering if they are not trying to develop the aesthetic sensibility or even moral character of their pupils, rather than teach them about language. And more recently, there has been a further reaction against an exclusive reliance on creative writing, and a feeling that a more structured approach is required. But it is often not clear what this approach should be. One obvious reason for the neglect of language work in teacher training is the lack of appropriate material. There are many introductions to linguistics on the market, but these are not usually designed for educationalists' interests. (An exception is Crystal, 1976.) Neither are there many suitable courses on language for educationalists, although appropriate syllabuses have now been proposed for student teachers and teacher trainers (HMSO, 1975), and the Open University offers two courses on language in education (PE232 and E263).

The approach taken in this book is that educationalists and sociologists of education should have a clear understanding of some of the central concepts of recent work in sociolinguistics, in so far as these are relevant to language in education. It is reasonable to believe that certain educational problems could be handled more successfully if teachers, and also educational researchers, had a clearer understanding of the sociolinguistic forces at work in schools and classrooms, of the ways in which language varies within a speech community, and of the attitudes which such language variation inevitably provokes. Such an understanding requires (a) attention to the observed details of language use in schools and classrooms. How do teachers and pupils actually talk to each other? But it also requires (b) a coherent framework to make sense of such observations. Observations are of no interest in themselves, unless we can relate them to general principles of language use in social contexts. These are the two points which the rest of the book tries to illustrate in detail.

2

Some basic
sociolinguistic
concepts

There has been much debate in educational and sociological circles since the mid-1960s about the precise relationship between education and language. One question often asked is: Does a child's language affect his success or failure at school? And if so, how? Many people believe that a child's language is a crucial cause of his educational success or failure. Another question often asked is: How does a teacher's language affect his pupils' learning? The aim of this chapter is to provide the reader with some of the basic sociolinguistic concepts necessary to understand the kinds of relationships which exist between language and educational processes. (By *sociolinguistics* I simply mean studies of language and how it is used in different social contexts, such as homes, factories, schools and classrooms.) Disentangling basic concepts is not merely an academic exercise, but essential to anyone who wants to understand the issues involved in the debate. What precisely is meant, for example, by the often quoted phrase: 'Educational failure is linguistic failure'? Does this phrase, in fact, make sense? Is there any precise meaning which can be attached to assertions that some pupils are 'linguistically inadequate'? And what would constitute evidence for such assertions?

2.1 Language and attitudes to language

The first distinction it is crucial to be clear about is the distinction between language itself and the deeply entrenched *attitudes* and *stereotypes* which most people hold about language.

It is difficult to overestimate the importance of people's attitudes and beliefs about language. It is almost impossible, for example, to hear someone speak, without immediately drawing conclusions, possibly very accurate, about their social-class background, level of education and what part of the country they come from. We hear language through a powerful filter of social values and stereotypes. As a precise example of what I mean by *linguistic stereotypes*, consider this fragment from a recorded classroom lesson which was based on a discussion of examples of dialect speech. The pupils have a transcript in front of them.

> **Teacher**: You can see on the bottom of your sheet, 'We ain't got no money.' That is typically a London accent – the tendency to drop the aitch off the front of words, d'you see? It's a lazy way of speaking.

Just these few comments embody several pieces of confused and dangerous linguistic folklore. The first is the *moral* censure ('lazy') which is attributed to a regional or social dialect feature. The second is the way this moral disapproval is backed up with pseudo-linguistic arguments. In the example the teacher quotes, there is nowhere to 'drop an aitch' from! The teacher may mean that 'ain't' is related to the standard form 'haven't'. But we cannot make the form standard by saying 'hain't'! 'Ain't' is now simply a dialect form of the negative. But 'dropping aitches' is a linguistic stereotype which is widely believed to characterize London speech, and it is thought to be 'lazy' or 'slovenly'. In fact, dropping of word-initial 'aitch' is found in the casual speech of educated speakers from most parts of the

25

country. The fragment also reveals other confusions: between spoken and written language; and between 'accent' or pronunciation and nonstandard grammar (e.g. the double negative). But we will leave these for the moment (see further Chs 2.3 and 4.1).

The point is that British people are very sensitive to the *social* implications of dialect and accent, and the characteristic speech of our large cities, especially Birmingham, east London, Liverpool, Newcastle and Glasgow, is often regarded as 'slovenly' and 'ugly'. Giles (1971) carried out experiments in which people listened to standard and regional dialects. In fact, they heard the same speaker using different language varieties, but they did not know this! Speakers of SE were *perceived* as more ambitious, more intelligent, more self-confident and more reliable. Such judgements may be manifestly unfair, but it is an important *social* fact that people judge a speaker's intelligence, character and personal worth on the basis of his or her language. We ought to be aware of the power of such social stereotyping.

It has been confirmed in many other studies, and is probably obvious from everyday experience, that a speaker's language is often a major influence on our impression of his or her personality. In particular it has been shown (in a Canadian study) that teachers evaluate pupils academically on the basis of their voices, and also their physical appearance, even when they have available relevant academic work on which to form their judgements, such as written compositions and art work (Seligman *et al.*, 1972). That is, a teacher may base serious systematic judgements about a pupil's intellectual abilities on totally irrelevant information. It is important for teachers to be aware that this tendency to linguistic stereotyping can mean that pupils may 'look and sound intelligent', and therefore to be aware of the misleading clues often used in evaluating them.

As a more detailed example of the weight people often attach to superficial features of language, consider this extract from an interview I recorded with two Edinburgh schoolgirls, aged 14. We were discussing a tape-recording of some dialect speech.

26

R: Well, they sound sort of as if they weren't very well brought up theirselves, the way they were talking.

MS: Mmhm – what are you thinking of in particular?

H: Their grammar's pretty awful.

MS: What's pretty awful about it?

H: *It only sort of went in a little bit.* (Quoting from recording.)

MS: What's wrong with that?

H: Well, you don't sort of say that, do you?

MS: Well, what in particular?

H: It's bad English.

MS: Why?

H: Well, it just sounds bad English.

MS: Which bit of it then, or is it all . . .?

H: It only *sort of* went in.

MS: So, you don't say *sort of*?

H: I keep saying *sort of*, yeah, but you're not meant to say *sort of*.

MS: Well, I mean you said, em, *you don't sort of say that*, I think.

H: I know – you're not meant to say that sort of thing – and I know I shouldn't.

MS: Why not?

H: It just doesn't sound right. It sounds as though you're Tarzan – Me Tarzan you Jane – Me speak English – sort of – I'm saying it again, aren't I?

MS: Well, don't you think it's quite a useful expression?

H: You get into the habit of using it, I won't say it again. I'll persevere and I won't say it. You get used to saying it if you hear other people saying it – you know you sort of – I'll never do it! – you associate that sort of thing with people who haven't really been taught to say it better.

The girls interpret the language of the tape as evidence that the speakers have been badly brought up, and are not far off the level of an (intellectually?) primitive Tarzan. But, when they are pressed, all they seem to be objecting to is the use of *sort of*. This is an expression which H herself uses constantly in the extract (in spite of her efforts not to!) and which most people use in informal conversation. Again, *sort of* is a feature of language which has acquired the status of a stigmatized stereotype. What are we to think, though, of an educational system which has so tied this girl in knots over a small and superficial linguistic item?

I conducted this interview as part of a series of discussions with Edinburgh children. I asked them to listen to recordings of boys from east London, and asked them to comment on what they heard. (The children did not know where the speakers came from or who they were.) One of the most striking things was the way in which the children singled out isolated features of speech as particularly reprehensible. These included the use of *you know* and *we was*. In general, the children tended to be hyperconscious of a very few stigmatized features, which were therefore made to carry a great weight of social significance. The recordings often elicited quite unjustified extrapolations like: 'He sounds like a skinhead from his voice.' Such is the power of linguistic stereotypes!

Some teachers might like to carry out such an experiment for themselves. It could form the topic of a lesson in English, or social science. The teacher could record people with different accents and dialects from the radio or television or from real life, and discuss with pupils why some speakers sound 'posh' or 'educated' or 'working class', and why such judgements may be very misleading.

There is evidence that such stereotypes are transmitted at least partly by schools. Very little work has been done on institutional attitudes to language, but Milroy and Milroy (1974, and in prep.) have done work on teachers' attitudes to language in Northern Ireland. They have evidence that colleges of education are particularly sensitive to such linguistic attitudes, that they screen applicants for acceptability of speech, and that they attempt subsequently to 'improve' candidates' speech. And in Glasgow, Macaulay (1978) interviewed about fifty teachers; he found that almost a third of them thought that the school should try to change the way pupils speak. Some teachers implied that because some children could not use the

28

language of the school, they were therefore less 'able' – thus basing far-reaching intellectual judgements on children's speech. (Chs 3 and 4 will explore fully whether such judgements have any basis.) Such findings about teachers' attitudes to speech are, for the present, rather impressionistic, but they could be corroborated or modified by anyone reading this book from his or her own classroom observations. It would be most important, for example, to see whether comments made by teachers in interviews correspond to the way they actually attempt to modify their pupils' language in the classroom.

It is clear at any rate that schools in our society have always been very sensitive to the social meaning of different language varieties. In some extreme social situations, children have actually been forbidden to speak their own language altogether, and even punished for using their native language in schools. This has been true in the past in Britain for Welsh and Scots Gaelic speakers (Trudgill, 1974, p. 134) and in the USA for American Indian children (Hymes, 1972). These may only be extreme and explicit examples of the disapproval of children's language often found in schools today. Scots Gaelic is now used in primary schools in north-west Scotland, and Welsh is actively encouraged in Welsh schools and is probably on the increase as a second language (Sharp, 1973). But in the very recent past in Wales, prisoners have been forbidden to speak Welsh to visitors (*The Times*, 28 April 1972). It is important to appreciate that language differences can provoke strong feelings of language loyalty and group conflict, and are therefore often a critical factor in education.

What is to be done?

One of the most important tasks in teacher training and in teaching pupils about language is to undermine such stereotypes. In itself, language diversity is no news to teachers: it is often all too evident in many schools. We require a way of making sense of the different kinds of diversity: geographical, ethnic, social and stylistic. (A detailed framework for under-

29

standing language diversity is provided by the companion reader to this book.) However, we require more than a mere understanding in principle.

One approach which has been proposed (for example, by Trudgill, 1975a) is called 'appreciation of dialect differences'. Trudgill argues that we should try to change people's attitudes, not their language (p. 69), and that we should try to increase people's tolerance of different accents and dialects (p. 101). This is important as far as it goes, and it is true that increased understanding can often lead to tolerance. But it is probably necessary also to attack the stereotypes directly, and to show up the mechanisms which transmit linguistic attitudes.

It is common, for example, for varieties of language and therefore their speakers to be identified on the basis of the kind of isolated and superficial features illustrated above. It is when such superficial features of accent or dialect are lumped together as 'bad English' and used in order to attach categoric labels to people that real violence can be done. Readers will be familiar with many labels for linguistic, social and ethnic groups. One British example is the term *teuchtar*, which is used pejoratively in Scotland to refer to Gaelic speakers or Highlanders.

This book is intended for teachers and student teachers, but it should provide much material for teaching pupils about language. A discussion of linguistic stereotypes can lead naturally to a more general discussion of how people are labelled as 'dull', 'adolescent', 'delinquent' or 'immigrant', and how such labels can influence how these people are perceived and treated.

2.2 The primitive language myth

Having now distinguished sharply between attitudes to language and language itself, let us look at some features of languages and dialects.

It is accepted by linguists that no language or dialect is inherently superior or inferior to any other, and that all languages and dialects are suited to the needs of the community they serve. A notion that one dialect is, say, more aesthetically pleasing than another is, as we have already seen, a culturally learned notion which generally reflects the social prestige of the dialect speakers, and not inherent properties of the dialect itself. The social prestige of groups of speakers, as it were, rubs off on their language.

Linguists long ago dispelled the myth that there are primitive tribes who speak 'primitive languages' with only 200–300 words, and simple grammar. It is now known that there is no correspondence at all between simplicity of material culture and simplicity of language structure, and all the world's languages have been shown to have vastly complex grammatical systems. However, the primitive language myth often lives on in a pernicious form, in the unfounded belief that the language of low-income groups in rural or urban industrial areas is somehow structurally 'impoverished' or 'simpler' than SE. There is no linguistic basis for such a belief. Fieldwork in urban and rural areas of Britain and the USA has demonstrated in detail that such dialects are inherently systematic and rule-governed, deeply organized systems of great complexity.

It is true, of course, that some languages are *functionally* more highly developed than others. Thus English is an international language, with a highly standardized writing system and is used in a wide range of functions from everyday casual conversation to writing scientific papers. Many hundreds of the world's languages have no writing systems and cannot therefore serve the same range of functions (Stubbs, 1980). It is also clear that the native language of an Amazonian Indian is unlikely to be well suited to discuss civil engineering. It is well known that languages reflect, in their vocabulary, the needs and interests of their speakers. Thus English does not need many different words for snow (which Eskimo has) or several dozen words for camel (which Arabic has).

None of these points, however, affect the central issue that all languages and dialects are vastly complex structural systems. (This will be illustrated further in Ch. 4.1.)

2.3 Standard and nonstandard English

I have already used terms such as *standard language* and *dialect* without discussing what they mean. Such terms are in common use, and although people often think their meaning is obvious, they turn out to be rather elusive. The definition of SE is complex, but it is important to give a rather careful and detailed definition, because SE has a special place in the education system in Britain. There are therefore several topics discussed elsewhere in this book which depend on a consistent definition. For example, there is the potential confusion between dialect and style (Ch. 1.2), the common confusion between restricted code and nonstandard English (Ch. 3), and the question of the relationship between Caribbean varieties of English and British English (Ch. 4.5).

Terminology and a preliminary definition

Several terms are used for SE including 'BBC English', the 'Queen's English' and 'Oxford English'. These terms are not very precise, and the third in particular is very out of date in its assumptions about British society. But they do no harm if they are not taken too literally. Another term, however, does not refer to the same thing at all. This is 'Received Pronunciation' (RP). This is a socially prestigious accent, and refers only to pronunciation, whereas SE refers to a dialect defined by grammar and vocabulary. There is a peculiar relationship between RP and SE. All users of RP speak SE: this is not logically necessary, but merely a fact about language in Britain. On the other hand, only a few speakers of SE use RP. For example, I speak SE with a regional west of Scotland accent. There is, in fact, no standard accent of English.

A fairly satisfactory preliminary definition of SE can be provided simply by listing examples of its main uses. SE is the variety of English which is normally used in print, and more generally in the public media (hence BBC English), and used by most educated speakers most of the time. It is the variety used in the education system and therefore the variety taught to learners of English as a foreign language. These examples tell any native speaker roughly what is meant by SE. On the other hand, they leave unclear whether SE is a predominantly written variety, and whether it is a prescriptive norm imposed by the education system or a description of the language which some people actually use.

Dialect and style

There is one widespread confusion which is easily disposed of. SE is a dialect, and like any other dialect there is stylistic variation within it. That is, SE may be either formal or casual and colloquial. The following sentences are all SE:

I have not seen any of those children.
I haven't seen any of those kids.
I haven't seen any of those bloody kids.

Speakers of SE can be as casual, polite or rude as anyone else, and can use slang, swear and say things in bad style or bad taste. This all has to do with stylistic variation or questions of social etiquette, and not with dialect. The following sentence is not SE:

I ain't seen none of them kids.

It is not incorrect SE: it is simply not SE at all. The double negative, the use of *them* as a demonstrative adjective and the use of *ain't*, are perfectly regular grammatical features which characterize many nonstandard dialects of British English. Vocabulary can also be regional and nonstandard: for example, *bairns* is regionally restricted to Scotland and northern England.

Regional versus social dialects

One important point about SE is that it is not regionally restricted as nonstandard dialects are. There is some regional variation between the SE used in England, Scotland, Wales and

Ireland, but very much less than in nonstandard varieties. In fact, there is a remarkably uniform international SE. Again there are small differences among the standard varieties used in Britain, North America, South Africa, Australia, New Zealand and the Caribbean. But the differences (in vocabulary, grammar and spelling) are minor given its very large number of speakers over an enormous geographical area.

It follows that SE is not a regional or geographical dialect. It is a social dialect: that dialect which is used by almost all 'educated' speakers. It is intuitively obvious that there is much more variation in the language used by working-class people in Britain than by middle-class people. Thus two businessmen from Aberdeen and Exeter would have little difficulty in understanding each other; but two farm labourers from Aberdeen and Exeter would speak very differently. Trudgill (1975a) diagrams the relation between social and regional diversity as follows:

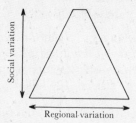

As we move up the social-class scale, there is less regional variation in dialect, though even right at the top there is still a little.

Standard, written and spoken English

There is stylistic variation within both spoken and written SE. However, spoken English is more variable due to the convention that most written (certainly printed) English is fairly formal. A very simple example of this is the convention against using forms such as *don't*, *doesn't* and *isn't* in printed books. This rather crude diagram illustrates several related points:

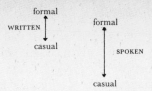

This is intended to indicate that spoken and written SE are (a) partly separate, but (b) overlapping. There is (c) variation in both, but (d) more variation in the spoken form. It shows that (e) the most formal written English is more formal than the most formal spoken, and (f) conversely with casual spoken English. And finally (g) as spoken English becomes more formal, it moves closer to written English.

If we add a nonstandard dialect, the following diagram represents further complications:

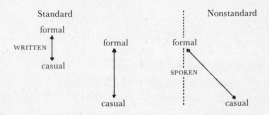

This is intended to indicate (a) that all written language is on the standard side of the line, and (b) that as nonstandard English becomes more formal, it moves towards SE, and may or may not coincide with SE.

The very strong social convention that all printed English is standard means that only occasional examples of dialect poetry and the like get into print. If a language is highly standardized, this implies in fact that it has a written form. This is because standardization implies deliberate codification and planning of the language by dictionary makers, grammar-book writers and the like. This brings us to the special relationship between SE and the education system, for it is the education system which is a powerful instrument for promoting such codified norms of language.

Usage versus prescription

People, including dictionary makers and schoolteachers, observe what they think is good usage. This may well be a mixture of local prejudice about what is a 'good accent', sometimes outdated norms of educated usage, and notions of written or even literary language which may be inappropriate to spoken English. On this basis they may formulate rules which may become quite rigid. Once established, such rules can become self-perpetuating. SE is used by prestigious people for prestigious purposes. The prestige of the speakers rubs off on the language, and the circle continues. SE, the social élite who use it, and the public functions it serves become inseparable.

Different types of definition

I have now used by implication several different types of definition of SE. SE is most closely related to regional dialects spoken in the south-east of England. This looks like a *geographical* definition. But, as I have pointed out, SE is no longer regionally restricted. In fact, this is a disguised *historical* definition: SE developed historically out of a dialect used in London, especially in the court. This shows in turn the need for a *social* definition. Historically SE spread because of the prestige of its users, and is now the social dialect used by educated middle-class speakers from all over Britain (and with minor variations in many other countries). I have also used a *functional* definition. SE is the variety used in print, in education and as an international language. These definitions are not prescriptive: they do not say who ought to use SE for what purposes. They are descriptive: they describe certain social facts which govern how it is, as a matter of fact, used. These conventions are socially and politically loaded, but I have not passed any judgement on whether they are desirable or not.

However, it is easy to see how the borderline between a descriptive and a prescriptive definition breaks down. The reason for one further confusion should now be clear. SE is prestigious and because of its speakers and its uses it is simply more visible than other varieties. The very fact that it is the variety used in print makes it more visible. People therefore come to think of SE as *the* language. They confuse one socially predominant dialect with 'the English language'. This is clearly an extreme idealization, since the whole point of my discussion has been that English is a cluster of many different styles and dialects. This is one way in which a descriptive definition turns into a prescriptive one. Other varieties may simply be defined out of existence as 'bad English' or 'not real English'.

The sociolinguistic view of SE is often misrepresented. It is often said, for example, that sociolinguists argue that SE is just another dialect, like any other, with no privileged position. This is not so. It is quite evident that SE holds a special position. What sociolinguists emphasize is that this special position is not due to any linguistic superiority. It is due to a complex of historical, geographical and social factors which I have tried briefly to summarize.

For further details and many examples of social and regional variation in standard and nonstandard varieties of English, see Hughes and Trudgill (1979) and Trudgill and Hannah (1982). For further discussion of the relation between spoken and written English, see Stubbs (1980).

2.4 Language structure and language use

A native speaker of a language knows, largely unconsciously, a vast number of facts about his language. Much of this knowledge involves the ability to understand complex grammatical relationships within sentences. For example, given two sentences such as:

| The teacher asked John to go | (1) |
| The teacher told John to go | (2) |

a speaker of English knows that they mean almost the same thing, except that *asked* implies more politeness than *told*. But contrast these two sentences:

The teacher asked John what to do (3)
The teacher told John what to do (4)

We know that, although the surface grammar of (3) and (4) is identical, the sentences express different underlying relations. In (3) it is the teacher who will do something. In (4) it is John who will do something. Our knowledge of our language comprises awesomely complex knowledge of such surface and underlying grammatical relationships: that is, knowledge about language *structure*. If you are unconvinced that such knowledge *is* awesomely complex, consider further such examples as these:

I expected John to be examined by the doctor (5)
I persuaded John to be examined by the doctor (6)
I expected the doctor to examine John (7)
I persuaded the doctor to examine John (8)

How do we know that (7) is a paraphrase of (5)? But that (8) is not a paraphrase of (6)? We have no trouble understanding such sentences and the relations between them. But you would find it very difficult indeed to make explicit exactly why we understand sentences in this way. Recall, then, that any dialect of any language is based on many hundreds of such structural relationships.

There is much more to language, however, than grammatical structure. A speaker of English knows that both (9) and (10) are grammatically normal:

Give me that comic (9)
Could I have that comic, please (10)

But he also knows that (9) and (10) are *used* in quite different *social situations*. (9) and (10) have the same referential meaning: they could refer to the same event. But they clearly have quite different social meanings. A teacher might say (9) to a pupil. The pupil might later say (10) to the teacher. A main task for sociolinguists is to specify such relationships between the use of language and different social situations and social relationships.

Grammatical and communicative competence

The ability to speak a language is not, therefore, only the ability to produce grammatical sentences. Hymes (1967) sums it up neatly: 'A child capable of using all grammatical utterances, but not knowing which to use, not knowing even when to talk and when to stop, would be a cultural monstrosity.' Knowing a language thus involves knowing how to say the right thing in the appropriate style at the right time and place. It involves complex knowledge of how to say what, to whom, when and where. This knowledge of how to *use* language *appropriately* in *social situations* is termed *communicative competence*. (The term is Hymes's.) Although children have acquired the bulk of a vast complex grammatical system by the time they begin school at 4 or 5 years, they continue to acquire the sociolinguistic system until well into their teens or beyond.

Language varieties

Different language is used in different situations, so we can say that a language is not a uniform object. It is a basic principle of sociolinguistics that there are no single-style speakers (Labov, 1972b). That is, everyone is multidialectal or multistylistic, in the sense that they adapt their style of speaking to suit the social situation in which they find themselves. It is intuitively clear, for example, that a boy does not speak in the same way to his teachers, his parents, his girlfriend or his friends in the play-ground. Imagine the disastrous consequences all round if he did! His way of talking to his teacher will also change according to the topic: answering questions in class or organizing the school sports. People adapt their speech according to the person they are talking to and the point behind the talk. These are social rather than purely linguistic constraints.

As a more general example of what I have in mind by language varieties, consider the following rather mixed bag of different varieties or styles of English, spoken and written: BBC English, Cockney, officialese, journalese, lecture, church sermon. These language varieties differ along several dimensions, notably regional/geographical, social class and functional/contextual. But their description involves questions of the same order: who says what? to whom? when? where? why? and how? In addition, more than one dimension is typically involved in any one of the varieties. For example, 'BBC English' implies not only that the speaker is likely to come from a certain region (southern Britain) and belong to a certain social class (educated middle class), but also implies a relatively formal social situation (probably not casual conversation in a pub). Some of what I have listed as language varieties might be thought of rather as speech situations. But speech and situation are not entirely separable in this way. For example, it is not simply that certain social situations demand that a teacher 'gives a pupil a dressing down'. By 'giving a pupil a dressing down' the teacher may create a certain social situation!

Note the importance of the concept of language variation when discussing children's language. A teacher may tend to think of a child's language in a stereotyped way, as though the child was a one-variety speaker. But the teacher typically sees the child in only a narrow range of social situations in the classroom, and may forget that the child also controls *other* language varieties. In other words, many teachers are unaware that all speech communities use ranges of different language varieties in different social contexts; yet this is an elementary sociolinguistic fact. Conversely, many teachers maintain the fiction that there is only one 'best' English for all purposes, and that this is the only English proper to the classroom. Yet a moment's thought or observation will convince any teachers that they themselves use many varieties of language throughout the day, depending on the purpose or context of the communication. This is not reprehensible, implying a chameleon-like fickleness, but a basic sociolinguistic fact about language use all over the world.

Correctness or appropriateness?

The concept that different language varieties are suited to different situations can be summed up in the distinction which is often drawn between correctness and appropriateness of language. Many of us were taught at school some version of the doctrine of correctness: that 'good English' means grammatically correct SE; and that the use of colloquialisms, slang or nonstandard forms is 'bad English'. No linguist would nowadays take this *prescriptive* attitude. Contemporary linguistics is strictly *descriptive*: it describes what people do, and does not try to prescribe what they ought to do. This does not mean, of course, that 'anything goes'. If a pupil writes a letter to a prospective employer which is full of colloquialisms or nonstandard forms, he will have to be warned of the conventions of English usage. It is not that such forms are wrong in any absolute sense, but that they are considered inappropriate to this social occasion – applying for a job.

Macaulay (1978) interviewed personnel managers, a careers officer and the director of an employment agency in Glasgow, to investigate the importance employers attach to speech in interviewing school leavers for jobs. He discovered that most employers feel that speech is important and may be crucial at the interview stage. Only a few of those interviewed said that an applicant's accent was important, but there were many complaints about 'slovenly speech'. There is no reason why such views about language should not be discussed openly with pupils in schools: in the English classroom, for example. As Macaulay says, social judgements about language, particularly about accent, are treated as a taboo subject even less mentionable than sex or money.

To say that a piece of language is 'wrong' is therefore to make a judgement relative to a social situation. It may be felt just as inappropriate to use colloquialisms and regional dialect forms in a job interview, as it is to use very formal language over a drink with some friends in a pub. In the first instance one is likely to be thought uncouth, impolite, socially gauche or uneducated.

(However unjustified such judgements may be, it is only fair to warn pupils that people *do* base harsh social judgements on surface characteristics of other people's speech. The ultimate aim here must be to make more people more tolerant of linguistic diversity.) In the second case one risks being thought aloof, stand-offish, 'lah-de-dah' or a bit of a snob.

It follows, then, that *within* SE (as I showed in Ch. 2.3) there is stylistic variation according to social context. Thus SE has formal and informal styles in both writing and speech. So, the use of colloquial forms, slang or swear words are all quite normal *within* SE. They simply define the style as informal: they do not define it as nonstandard. As a speaker of SE moves between different social situations, he or she will *style-shift*. But precisely the same functions may be served by other speakers shifting between dialects. For example, many West Indian children in Britain are *bidialectal*, using a form of creole English in the home and a more formal language variety, much closer to SE, in school (see Ch. 4.5).

A teacher may often find that he or she wants both to defend some controversial form (e.g. split infinitives) because it is nowadays in widespread usage, but also to warn pupils not to use it when, say, writing a job application. In other words, the question 'What is correct English?' is too oversimple to answer. (Mittins, 1969, gives an entertaining and sensible discussion of this.) To say, therefore, that someone's English is 'wrong' is to make not a linguistic, but a sociolinguistic judgement.

Production and comprehension

Suppose then that a teacher observes that a child uses language inappropriate (in the teacher's terms) for the classroom. Is this because the child does not know the forms the teacher thinks appropriate? Or because the child knows the forms but does not realize that it is appropriate to use them in this situation? If a teacher observes that a child never *produces* a particular linguistic item (word, sentence-type, etc.) this may mean several things: (a) that the child neither knows nor understands the item; (b) that the child *understands* the item, but never *uses* it in his own speech; or (c) that the child both knows and uses the item, but the teacher has never observed the child in a situation where the child finds it appropriate and necessary to use it. We all have a passive knowledge of many aspects of our language, words and constructions, which we understand but never actively use. An adult's passive vocabulary, for example, typically includes several hundred words which he understands but does not use. And most of us can understand certain styles of language, say the language of the courtroom, which we could not, however, competently use ourselves. Similarly, young children understand many things that their parents say to them long before they can actively produce the same items. That is, speakers have asymmetrical linguistic systems: they can perceive and understand linguistic distinctions which they do not (or cannot) themselves make.

A simple experiment by Labov (1969) illustrates this distinction sharply. He asked Negro youths in the USA, who were speakers of nonstandard dialect, simply to repeat the sentence: 'I asked Alvin if he knows how to play basketball.' The boys were unable to repeat this SE sentence, and instead regularly produced a nonstandard sentence such as 'I axt Alvin does he know how to play basketball.' That is, they produced a version which differed from the original in details of surface grammar. Clearly, the boys had *understood* the *meaning* of the original sentence, since they could immediately and correctly translate the sentence into their own dialect. Yet they could not *produce* the surface grammar of the target sentence. We must therefore be very careful before we equate the inability to *use* a particular grammatical form with the inability to *understand* it or the concept which underlies it.

2.5 The implication of such distinctions

These distinctions between different aspects of linguistic competence are not merely academic. They show at once that any claim to relate 'language' directly to 'education' is almost certain

43

to be so oversimple as to be meaningless. Is one talking about: comprehension or production? language structure or language use? prescriptive norms of correctness or appropriateness to social context? grammatical or communicative competence? the child's language itself or the school's attitudes to his language? It should already be clear how oversimple it is to say that a child's language *directly* determines his success or failure at school. The child *uses* different *varieties* of language in different *social situations*, say home and school. The teacher may (rightly or wrongly) regard the child's language as *inappropriate* to the classroom. The child's language may also provoke negative *attitudes* in the teacher, perhaps because the child speaks a low-prestige dialect. These attitudes may be transmitted to the child. Even if the teacher expresses no overt disapproval of the child's language, the teacher's own language may still be different from the child's in the direction of prestige varieties, and this in itself may be an implicit condemnation of the child's language. The child will be aware that people with more prestige and authority than him speak differently, and may draw his own conclusions. Such a complex of sociolinguistic factors may lead cumulatively to educational problems for a child.

Thus a child's language may be a *disadvantage* in his educational progress: not because his language is itself 'deficient', but because it is different. These distinctions may seem initially to recall the Feiffer cartoon which runs:

> I used to think I was poor. Then they told me I wasn't poor, I was *needy*. Then they told me it was self-defeating to think of myself as needy, I was *deprived*. Then they told me deprived was a bad image, I was *underprivileged*. Then they told me underprivileged was overused. I was *disadvantaged*. I still haven't got a dime, but I have a great vocabulary.

But it is important to ask just how the disadvantage arises. Is it 'in' children's language? Or does it arise rather from people's attitudes to language differences? If you believe that children's language can be 'deficient', then you might be tempted to try and 'improve' their language in some way. If you believe, on the contrary (as this book argues), that the concept of language deficit does not make much sense, and that there is nothing wrong with the language of any normal child, then you will probably believe that schooling should not interfere with children's dialects. This is not to say that teachers should not try to develop and extend their pupils' competence in different varieties of language. A view that all dialects are valuable is quite compatible with attempts to extend the functional range of children's language. After all, we are all developing our competence in different styles of language throughout our whole lives. And if you believe (as this book also argues) that linguistic disadvantage arises largely from people's intolerance and prejudice towards language differences, then you will probably try to change people's attitudes to language (see Ch. 2.1).

Having begun to disentangle some sociolinguistic concepts, we are now in a position to discuss some specific studies of language in education.

3

Bernstein's theory of restricted and elaborated codes

It is an important social fact that working-class (WC) children do not do as well at school as middle-class (MC) children. This is not to say that no WC children are successful in the formal education system. But a WC child has much less chance than a MC child of, say, reaching university. This fact is not in dispute: it poses a problem for educationalists and demands an explanation. Nor is there any dispute over the fact that the language used by WC children is characteristically different from the language of MC children. This is an elementary observation about sociolinguistic diversity in an industrialized society like Britain or the USA.

Much disagreement centres, however, on the interpretation of these two facts. Are they, for example, causally related? One type of theory which has been frequently proposed over the past ten years or so is that the difficulties of WC children at school are *caused* by their language. The WC child's language, according to such theories, is said to be somehow unsuitable for the type of intellectual or cognitive activities which are the basis of education. The gist of the argument over the next two chapters will be that such a proposition is, as yet, unproven. There is no firm evidence that differences in language are causally and directly related to differences in intellectual ability. Certainly, no one has yet satisfactorily explained precisely what features of a child's language contribute to his educational success. However, such theories are widely accepted by teachers and taught in colleges of education, and it is important to understand the issues involved. They are widely accepted because they have a certain immediate plausibility, and this is all the more reason for carefully examining the evidence said to support them.

Note for the present that alternative theories are still open, for example: the two facts are not causally related – they are both caused by something else – or, the two facts are related, but not directly.

3.1 The work of Basil Bernstein

The best known name in the language and education field is Basil Bernstein, who is Professor of Sociology of Education at London University. His views have filtered down, often in out-of-date or inaccurate formulations, through most colleges of education, and have entered staffroom folklore. Most British teachers have at least a passing acquaintance with the theories for which he is primarily known. These theories concern social-class differences in language, and propose causal relationships between a child's social class, his language and his success or failure at school. In particular, Bernstein is known for the concept of 'restricted' and 'elaborated' code, for the theory that some WC children may not have access to elaborated code, and for the theory that this partly explains their problems at school.

(The work of Bernstein and his colleagues is published in three volumes, *Class, Codes and Control*. To save space, I will refer to these as *CCC 1, 2* and *3*. *CCC 1* and *3* are Bernstein's own collected papers. *CCC 2* is mainly experimental work by his colleagues. The papers in *CCC 3* do not deal directly with language and will be referred to only briefly in later chapters. *CCC 1* is mostly easily available in a Paladin paperback, and my page references are to this (the 1973 edition containing a postscript by Bernstein which is not in the original 1971 edition). References to *CCC 2* and *3* are to hardback editions published by Routledge & Kegan Paul.)

In fact this particular question about educability (does a child's language affect his progress at school?) is, for Bernstein, only part of a much more general question which he calls the 'structure and process of cultural transmission' (*CCC 1*, p. 19). *Cultural transmission* is Bernstein's term for socialization. The problem is: How do children come to learn what is socially appropriate behaviour? How do they acquire the expectations, assumptions and ways of seeing the world of their family, friends or teachers? By using the term cultural transmission, Bernstein emphasizes that what the child acquires are 'symbolic orders': ways of organizing experience. This sounds very abstract, and it is. Bernstein has justifiably complained that his critics have frequently not recognized just which level of problem he is dealing with (*CCC 1*, p. 262). It should be clear simply from Bernstein's terms and concepts (e.g. 'codes', 'symbolic orders') that he is not just talking about social-class stratification and saying in a roundabout way that WC children do badly at school.

It is difficult to assess Bernstein's work for several practical reasons which it is best to clear out of the way at once. First, his views have altered in crucial respects since his first paper was published in 1958. It is reasonable of Bernstein to argue that where research leads is more important than where it started, but this provides a severe practical problem for readers. Bernstein has complicated this problem, for he has republished a collection of his papers (*CCC 1*), which span the years 1958 to 1973 and contain many contradictory statements. He has also published experimental papers (*CCC 2*) based on his early and now outdated theoretical position. He admits that this experimental work is based on a 'much coarser theoretical position' than he now holds (*CCC 2*, p. 36). There is therefore the danger that casual readers never get past the early papers which Bernstein now recognizes as inadequate statements of the complex relationships between language, social class and educability. Second, because of the social and educational implications of his work, his views have often been seized upon by others in support of language policies in education. In the course of this, Bernstein's views have often been oversimplified, misused or distorted. At certain points below, I comment on how some people have understood Bernstein, rather than on what he has himself said: this is the nature of the debate. Third, Bernstein's style is highly abstract, heavily loaded with sociological terms, and contains few examples of actual language in use. The work is therefore often difficult to understand.

3.2 Bernstein's early work

In the out-of-date version in which Bernstein's theories are most widely known, the argument runs thus. There are two different kinds of language, *restricted* and *elaborated* code, which are broadly related to the social class of speakers. MC speakers are said to use both codes, but some WC speakers are said to have access only to restricted code, and this is said to affect the way such speakers can express themselves and form concepts. This is claimed to be particularly important in education, since 'schools are predicated upon elaborated code' (*CCC 1*, p. 212). Few detailed examples of the codes were given, but elaborated code was said to be characterized by accurate and complex grammar, frequent use of prepositions, impersonal pronouns, passive verbs, and unusual adjectives and adverbs. Conversely, restricted code was said to be characterized by short, grammatically simple, often unfinished sentences; frequent use of short commands and questions, categoric statements ('Do as I tell you'); simple and repetitive use of conjunctions; rigid and limited use of adjectives and adverbs.

The theory is appealing because it appears to provide a *linguistic explanation* of why WC children are less successful than MC children at school. In this early version of the theory – *to which Bernstein no longer subscribes* – a *direct* relation was claimed between social class and the codes to which a speaker had access:

49

a crude correlation between forms of language and social class (*CCC 1*, p. 226). Since Bernstein no longer holds this view, and since it has been criticized in detail by others (see Ch. 3.6 for some references), I will not discuss it here.

What I will do, however, in order to point out some of the dangers in an unqualified acceptance of this type of position, is discuss an experimental study based on this early theoretical position. This will also allow me to give specific illustrations of some of the concepts discussed in Chapter 2, and to illustrate the need to develop sufficiently sophisticated sociolinguistic concepts to handle the relationships between language, social class and social context.

Hawkins's experiment

Consider, then, a much quoted experiment by Hawkins (1969) who set out to study the relationship between the language of 5 year old children and their social class (MC or WC). He divided over 300 children into MC and WC on the basis of the occupational and educational status of their parents. The children were then interviewed and given tasks to do. One task was to look at a series of four pictures showing some boys playing football, kicking a ball through a window, being shouted at by a man and running away. They then had to tell the story in the pictures. Hawkins quotes two 'slightly exaggerated' versions of the same story as told, respectively, by MC and WC children. That is, although he must have collected over 300 *actual* stories, he *invents hypothetical* illustrations for his argument – he gives no reason for this. (I will return later to this crucial lack of real linguistic data in Bernstein's work.) The two versions are as follows.

(1) Three boys are playing football and one boy kicks the ball and it goes through the window – the ball breaks the window and the boys are looking at it – and a man comes out – and shouts at them – because they've broken the window – so they run away – and then that lady looks out of her window – and she tells the boys off.

(2) They're playing football and he kicks it and it goes through there – it breaks the window and they're looking at it and he comes out and shouts at them because they've broken it – so they run away – and then she looks out and she tells them off.

Hawkins argues that the two stories differ in *elaboration* and in the amount of information communicated. (1) is *explicit* about what happens, but (2) cannot be understood without the pictures and therefore makes greater demands on the listener. This is because (1) uses many nouns to convey information, whereas (2) depends largely on pronouns. He argues further that these 'considerable differences' between WC and MC children's language 'may well have important *cognitive* consequences' (*CCC* 2, p. 91), since WC children have reduced possibilities of modification and qualification (you cannot modify a pronoun with an adjective). The data for these arguments are statistically significant differences in the numbers of nouns and pronouns used by the two groups of children.

This argument falls down in several ways. Consider this startling statement:

> The second of the versions makes enormous demands on the listener. It means that the context (i.e. the pictures) must be present if the listener is to understand who and what is being referred to. It assumes the listener can *see* the pictures. (*CCC* 2, p. 87.)

But the listener (researcher) *can* see the pictures! He does not need to be told explicitly who 'they' are, or where they kick the ball. Version (2) is perfectly *appropriate* in a situation in which there is no reason to use elaborated or explicit language. One can stand Hawkins's argument on its head and say that the WC version takes appropriate account of the listener's knowledge; while the MC version is full of redundant information. This is completely the opposite of Hawkins's conclusion: perhaps it is the MC children who are incapable of adapting their language to

51

the context, since they treat the researcher as someone who must have the most obvious things explained to him!

Where has Hawkins gone wrong? Principally, he crucially ignores the social context in various ways. He fails to discuss how language is adapted to its context of use (see Ch.2.4). He studies language use in an experimental interview setting, not natural language use. Perhaps the WC children were simply more overawed by the situation than the MC children: remember they were 5 years old! Using an experimental situation does not 'control' the context; it just provides a different context with different rules (see Ch. 5.3). Perhaps the WC children felt less at home than the MC ones, alone for half an hour with a strange adult; and perhaps they did not realize the verbal game they were being asked to play. As Wight (1975) says about such adult–child contexts: 'What can you tell a man about his picture that he can't already see and doesn't already know?' The experiment might indicate that young MC children were better at role-playing, that is, at pretending the researcher could not see the pictures. The fact that Hawkins fails to consider the context means that he fails to consider the crucial distinction between knowledge of language and use of language (see Ch. 2.4). It could well be that the WC children *knew how* to use elaborated language, and would do so if they thought it appropriate. But this situation failed to elicit such language. The experiment shows that the WC children *used* certain language; it does not show that they would not have used different language in different circumstances (if the listener had not known what was in the picture, for example).

Hawkins's experiment uncovers potentially interesting differences in the language of WC and MC children. But, due to the inadequacy of his sociolinguistic framework, he has no way of speculating sensibly on what the differences mean.

Note a most important point. Bernstein's own comments on this experiment are much more guarded and reasonable than the conclusions Hawkins draws in the original paper. Bernstein points out that differing use of explicit and implicit language does not mean that WC children do not have access to explicit,

52

elaborated language (*CCC 1*, p. 219). What the experiment shows is differences in the *use* of language *in a specific context*, and Bernstein maintains that it would not be difficult to imagine a context in which the WC children would produce speech rather like the MC ones. All the experiment shows is that this experimental context did not elicit elaborated language from the WC children. The generalization which is *warranted* is: 'the social classes differ in terms of the *contexts* which evoke certain linguistic realizations'. To repeat, however, we can draw no conclusions whatsoever about which contexts *do* elicit which styles of language in such children.

Eight years after his 1969 article, Hawkins (1977) published a full-length book (in a series edited by Bernstein) which presents a substantial reanalysis and reinterpretation of his 1969 data. In this book Hawkins takes, like Bernstein, a much more cautious line and admits that his earlier work had crucially ignored the social context and the functions of utterances in conversation. However, in being more cautious, Hawkins may have so weakened his claims that there is little left to argue with. For example, he drops all references to children's cognitive abilities, claiming simply that WC and MC children speak differently from each other in experimental situations. He also claims that the children talk differently because of speech differences in their home backgrounds (pp. 200 ff.). This would be interesting if it could be documented. But there is no observation to support the claim: only hypothetical interview data (pp. 64, 202). Mothers were asked how they *would* talk to their children in different situations.

Despite such limitations, the book is valuable. First, it is a warning that widely divergent interpretations can be placed on data about social-class variation in language use. Second, it demonstrates that everything is vastly more complex than a crude dichotomy between elaborated and restricted code often implies. Hawkins's analysis is careful and painstaking. What we are dealing with are differences in the relative frequency of items which all the children use: not with an absolute difference between two groups. However, it is precisely such data which can be taken as evidence against the codes theory. If there are no absolute differences, if it is all highly context-dependent and all a matter of relative frequencies in usage, then this provides no support for the concept of two discrete underlying codes.

Note one interesting suggestion from Bernstein about the relevance of such experimental situations to the school situation (*CCC 1*, p. 278). He argues that there is a broad analogy between experimental settings and the test situation in school: similar social assumptions underlie them. They are both situations in which the child is in an abnormal setting, isolated from other children, with an adult who provides minimal support, and where he must do tasks very different from what he is used to outside school. For reasons which are not yet known, MC children are more successful (i.e. do what teachers/experimenters want) in both such settings. One obvious conclusion to draw from this is, however, that it is schools which should change, not children. (Bernstein does not draw this conclusion.) One danger is, of course, that a strange or hostile experimental or test situation may be taken as evidence of a child's total linguistic ability (see Ch. 4.3). Bernstein does not make this mistake but it is something to guard against. These differing interpretations of the same data emphasize the need for extreme caution in drawing general conclusions about the relationships between language, social class and cognitive ability.

Note, then, that Bernstein no longer talks of a direct relation between language and social class. He uses two intervening concepts: (a) he distinguishes language from *use* of language; and (b) he distinguishes different social *contexts* in which language is used.

Language forms and language functions

Turner (1973, *CCC 2*) gives a precise linguistic example of this crucial point that it is not possible to make sense of social-class differences in language use unless one looks at the social contexts which control language. For example, one way of threatening someone is to use a grammatically complex utterance such

54

as: 'If you do that again, I'll hit you.' In an experiment with young children, Turner found that WC children used more threats, and therefore *more* grammatically complex language than MC children. Note also that this form of threat is grammatically very similar in form to rational appeals of the type: 'If you eat that now, you won't want your dinner.' These examples make clear the importance of not confusing grammatical complexity of *form* with the social *function* of the language. There is no simple correspondence between the complexity of language (e.g. at the grammatical level) and the complexity of functions, cognitive or social, which it serves.

In a relatively early paper (1965), Bernstein himself appears critically confused about the relation between linguistic form and cognitive processes. He quotes two short extracts of restricted code. These are the *only* examples of restricted code of more than a couple of sentences in length in the whole of *CCC 1*, so it is important to look at them closely. Here is one of them:

> It's all according like these youths and that if they get into these gangs and that they must have a bit of a lark around and say it goes wrong and that they probably knock someone off I mean think they just do it to be big getting publicity here and there. (*CCC 1*, p. 158)

Bernstein does not comment on the details of the extract, but says it will illustrate various points about restricted code: namely, that there is a 'rigid range of syntactic possibilities', leading to 'difficulty in conveying linguistically logical sequence and stress' (p. 157).

Note first that we have no information about the context of the language, except that the speaker is 17 years old. Nor are we given any information about the intonation, or changes in speed or stress which often structure and organize spoken language. Let us concentrate, however, on the words on the page. Clearly, the language is neither particularly memorable nor particularly effective. But it certainly does *not* show thoughts 'strung together like beads on a frame rather than following a planned

55

sequence' (p. 158) or any difficulties in handling a logical argument. There is *no* inability to convey an abstract argument involving hypothetical cases and interdependent propositions. (*If* some youths get in a gang *and if* something goes wrong *when* they are having a lark about, *then* someone might get killed.) There is no problem in understanding what is meant, as this translation into more formal (written) style indicates. Therefore, the language is not tied to its context. There is, therefore, no support for the contention that such language 'initiates and sustains . . . radically different . . . conditions of learning' (p. 157).

In his early papers, Bernstein claimed that restricted code has a 'logically simpler language structure' (*CCC 1*, p. 47) than elaborated code. This kind of statement (which confuses complexity of linguistic form with complexity of thought) is quite misleading and Bernstein no longer makes it. (Gazdar, 1979, provides a thorough analysis of this confusion.) But in later papers (e.g. 1973) he still insists that different forms of language have different cognitive effects, since they 'focus experience' in different ways (1973, p. 211). If, however, such statements cannot be related to actual language in use, then it is not clear what value they have.

3.3 Bernstein's later work (1973)

A major difference between Bernstein's earlier and later work is an increase in the depth of complexity and abstraction at which the theory is formulated. I will summarize the position which Bernstein proposes in 'Social class, language and socialization', his most recent paper (1973) in *CCC 1*. It is still the work on sociolinguistic codes for which Bernstein is best known, yet he has not published any papers on the codes since 1973, although he has published papers on other topics: a fact noted by several commentators. Nor has he published any overview which attempts to reconcile the contradictions in his work between 1958 and 1973.

In Bernstein's first published paper (1958) he talks of public and formal language (these terms were later changed to restricted and elaborated code respectively) and discusses these as observable speech varieties. And in the earliest paper on linguistic codes (1962) he implies that restricted and elaborated codes can be partly defined in terms of features of language structure (e.g. *CCC 1*, p. 93). An elaborated-code user has more alternatives to choose from, while a restricted code is more predictable in its syntactic choices. But by the 1965 paper quoted above, Bernstein no longer defines the codes as actual language varieties. They are defined as abstract frameworks at a psychological level of verbal planning, and 'only at this level could they be said to exist' (*CCC 1*, p. 154). Nevertheless, there is the implication that by inspecting actual extracts of speech, one can tell whether they are related to elaborated or restricted code (e.g. *CCC 1*, p. 158, and see the extract quoted and discussed above, p. 55). In the later work, then, the relation between the codes and what people actually say is defined as much more complex and abstract.

Bernstein now distinguishes between *sociolinguistic codes* (elaborated and restricted) and *speech variants* (elaborated and restricted) which realize the codes (*CCC 1*, p. 200). The codes are now defined as entirely abstract, underlying, interpretive procedures which 'generate' different speech variants in different contexts. Thus Bernstein no longer claims a direct relationship between a speaker's social class and the codes he uses. He has introduced two intervening concepts of speech variant and context.

Speech variants are not actual language either. They are defined as 'contextual constraints upon grammatical–lexical choices' (*CCC 1*, p. 200). No detailed specification is given of these choices, but it is implied (p. 203) that restricted speech variants are characterized by a reduced range of syntactic alternatives and a narrow range of lexis (vocabulary): that is, they are defined in the same way as codes earlier were. Consistent with this increase in abstraction, speech variants are not, however, defined in terms of linguistic forms, but in terms of *meanings*. Thus, elaborated speech variants are said (p. 202) to realize *universalistic* meanings, i.e. meanings which are *explicit* and not tied to a given context (p. 199). Conversely, restricted speech variants realize *particularistic* meanings which are *implicit* and take for granted many shared meanings between speaker and hearer. (Compare Bernstein's comments, quoted above, on the Hawkins experiment.) It will be clear that this increase in abstraction has led Bernstein a very long way from observable language forms.

In order to discover whether someone is an elaborated or restricted-code user, one has to look at the language he or she uses in what Bernstein calls the four critical socializing contexts (*CCC 1*, p. 206): *regulative*, e.g. being told off by mother; *instructional*, e.g. the classroom; *imaginative*, e.g. in play; and *interpersonal*, e.g. in talk with others where the child is made aware of emotional states. If the linguistic realizations of these four contexts are 'predominantly' in terms of restricted speech variants, then the deep structure of the communication is said to be a restricted code. Conversely for elaborated code.

Note one most important point which has caused much confusion. Codes are *defined* as abstract, underlying principles which regulate communication and generate speech. People do not speak codes, just as they do not speak grammar: both grammar and codes are abstract, underlying systems. It is therefore incoherent to refer to a child as a 'restricted-code speaker'. One can only talk of a child who tends to use restricted speech variants in certain contexts.

Bernstein further adds to the complexity of the theory by distinguishing two *family types* (p. 209). In *positional* families, there is said to be clear-cut definition of the status of different members of the family, as 'father', 'grandmother' and so on. In *person-centred* families these status distinctions are blurred in favour of members' unique characteristics. Bernstein claims, without giving any details, that the communication structure in these different family types is differently focused, such that we should expect restricted code in positional families and elaborated code in person-centred families (p. 211). He claims that both family types can be found in both MC and WC, but implies

that, at the present time, positional families are more characteristic of the WC.

What has Bernstein now said? What is the form of his theory?
He is attempting to formulate a theory which relates a child's
social class, family background, language use and cognitive
style. He still claims (*CCC 1*, p. 209) that access to the codes is
'broadly related to social class' and that there 'may well be
selective access to elaborated code' (p. 208); that is, some WC
speakers do not have access to elaborated code but most (?) MC
speakers have access to both. This is because (so runs his
argument) there is selective access to the role systems which
evoke the use of the codes (p. 208). Within positional families we
should 'expect' restricted code (p. 211). But both positional and
person-centred families are found in both WC and MC (p. 209).
Finally, to know if a given piece of language realizes restricted or
elaborated code, we should have to observe the language use
across the four critical socializing contexts – for an elaborated
speech variant (defined in terms of meanings, not observable
linguistic forms) may realize a restricted code, and vice versa.

From the way I have summarized this position, it will be clear
that I believe the theory is now formulated in such a way that no
testable claim is now being made. The model apparently being
proposed might be summarized thus:

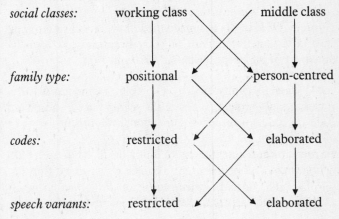

social classes: working class   middle class

family type: positional   person-centred

codes: restricted   elaborated

speech variants: restricted   elaborated

The arrows represent links between levels. The vertical columns represent 'expected' links. Thus WC families may be expected to be positional, but they may be person-centred. A positional family would lead one to expect code restriction, but if it should show (unspecified) signs of being person-centred, then the children might be able to switch codes.

When the theory is set out in this way, it becomes clear that it is not a real theory. No real predictions are made, for example, about which forms of family are related to which codes. All we have are 'expectations', unsupported by evidence. More important, it is not possible to refute such a theory from empirical evidence and observations. Genuine scientific theories make predictions that certain things (X) will happen under certain conditions, and that other things (Y) will not happen. The statement may involve specifying a statistical probability that X will occur: that is, a definable margin of error may be specified in the prediction. If Y does happen, the theory must be altered or abandoned, since it does not fit the facts. But Bernstein's model sets no real constraints on what may happen. An example of an elaborated speech variant may be expected to be a realization of elaborated code, but it may realize restricted code too. We can only know which code it realizes by investigating whether the critical socializing contexts of the speaker were predominantly characterized by restricted or elaborated speech variants – but this is uninvestigable.

Gordon (1981, p. 81) has made the following valiant attempt to give a succinct statement of what Bernstein has actually claimed in two papers published in 1970 and 1971:

social class → family structure → roles → modes of early socialization → roles . . . modes of perception . . . access to codes → codes → speech → educational attainment

An arrow indicates a claimed causal link; the dots indicate a link which is irremediably obscure in Bernstein's writings. Gordon notes that 'roles' occurs twice, and that the whole chain of causality is particularly obscure after the second occurrence. He notes also that the first and last entities in the chain are simply taken for granted.

The lack of linguistic analysis in Bernstein's work

The major limitation in Bernstein's work, from the point of view of its ability to make precise and testable statements, is the *almost total lack of linguistic exemplification* of his theories. Most of the papers are entirely abstract speculations with no precise linguistic data. Where Bernstein does provide brief linguistic examples and data, this is either (a) invented, i.e. imagined, fictional anecdotes (e.g. *CCC 1*, p. 201), or (b) hypothetical, e.g. mothers were asked what they would say *if* their child was naughty, or (c) taken from experimental test situations, as in Hawkins's experiment. There are no extended real-life examples of language use anywhere in Bernstein's papers: no more than a couple of conversational fragments in footnotes (e.g. *CCC 1*, p. 283), and no examples whatsoever of actual language use between mothers and children in the home or between teachers and pupils in the classroom.

3.4 Do the codes exist?

More radically, one has to question the linguistic evidence for the very existence of the codes. Early on in his work, Bernstein dropped the notion that the codes exist as observable language varieties. The only sense in which the codes could now be said to exist is as *hypothetical constructs* intended to explain social-class differences in language use and cognitive orientation. More precisely, then, are the codes a useful hypothesis? Do they, for example, explain the experimental evidence on language use which Bernstein and his colleagues have collected? And the answer is: No.

The experimental evidence that is said to support the concept of code is always of the form that one group of speakers (say MC) tends to use *more* of a certain kind of language than another group (WC). The differences are never absolute (cf. Hawkins's experiment). What the data display is one group using *more* of the *same* features than another group. *Both* groups use the same linguistic items (e.g. complex noun groups) but one group uses them more frequently. On the basis of these relative differences in frequency, Bernstein nevertheless argues for a sharp contrast between two underlying modes of speech: restricted and elaborated. On the basis of a measure of relative frequencies, however, a notion of a continuum might be more appropriate: a cline of continuously variable speech behaviour.

There is also a more fundamental worry over such counts of relative frequency in the use of linguistic items. Suppose in 5 minutes' speech a WC child uses simple pronouns most of the time (*he*, *she*, *it*, etc.) and just once uses a complex noun group (e.g. *the very old man*), then this proves that he or she *does* know how to use complex noun phrases, not that he or she doesn't. Statistical statements about language are therefore always evidence *against* fundamental differences in language capacity, not for them. All the empirical work (in *CCC 2*) shows is rather minor differences in relative frequency of some grammatical items, between WC and MC groups. Trudgill puts this succinctly:

> If we look at things from a purely linguistic point of view – all the theorizing of the past sixteen years appears to have reduced to evidence that, in situations more artificial and alien to them than to middle-class children, working-class children use a higher proportion of pronouns. Is this what it has been all about? (1975b)

Various writers (e.g. Trudgill, 1975b; Labov, 1969; Kochman, 1972) have for this reason suggested that Bernstein is here dealing with mere differences of style.

Bernstein may, however, have hit on a more important difference than this. It may be that in choosing characteristic styles of language, WC and MC speakers are reflecting different preferred modes of discussion and therefore different value systems about what it is important to elaborate and make explicit. Educationally, this would still be a very important thing to demonstrate. But still, one has to emphasize that value systems cannot be read unproblematically off statistical features of language use. And what one certainly cannot argue is that such language use constrains cognitive orientation in any absolute sense. Such statistical data are also evidence against the notion that language can constrain a speaker's thought, since one cannot be constrained by mere tendencies in one's language (cf. Jackson, 1974). What has to be explained is why WC children do not frequently *use* linguistic forms they quite clearly *know* (and which tend to be valued by teachers).

I am here drawing attention again to the distinction between knowledge of language and use of language (see Ch. 2.4). It is important to realize that Bernstein claims always to be talking about speech and therefore use of language. But one is still left with the complete lack of explanation, within the theory, for *why* different social groups *use* different forms of language in different contexts. There is, for example, no attempt to analyse the different values which different social groups place on different forms of language. In other words, the experimental evidence on differences between MC and WC speakers' use of language is important. But it is unclear how this empirical evidence is related, if at all, to the codes theory.

I am suggesting that Bernstein's theory has an unclear and unacceptable status. First, it is now formulated in a way which makes it untestable. Second, it has a loose, if not actually contradictory relationship to the experimental evidence said to support it. The experimental tests have uncovered interesting social-class differences in language use, but they are not tests of the theory. And the theory does not explain the experimental evidence.

3.5 Some possible confusions

Educationalists have often used Bernstein's work in support of educational policies. (It is clear *that* Bernstein's theories have educational implications, but no one seems quite clear just what these implications are!) Bernstein's work has been used, for example, to support the oversimple statement that 'educational failure is linguistic failure'. This is unfair to Bernstein. It is true that the most apparent concomitant of educational failure is often a pupil's language. This is what is immediately visible and audible to the teacher, and often the only evidence of academic ability that a teacher has to go on. But beyond a pupil's language, Bernstein emphasizes a highly complex set of factors: family background, social class and so on. The child's language, in so far as this is observable to teachers, is literally the most superficial aspect of his sociolinguistic competence.

It is important to make explicit some features of language which must not be confused with the notion of restricted code (cf. Trudgill, 1975a, Ch. 5). First, it is clear that the mismatch between school and pupil is not simply due to a pupil's lack of words. A child may not have a well-developed vocabulary, but this cannot constrain his thinking in any absolute way, since he can simply learn more words (as we all do all our lives). Any vocabulary can be expanded, and a child with a poor vocabulary may still be a fluent speaker if he has other linguistic strategies to compensate. Nor are the child's problems due to impoverished, simple or deficient grammar. There is no evidence that the language structure used by socially disadvantaged groups is less complex than that, say, of SE (see Chs. 2.2 and 4.1). Nor are such educational problems due directly to nonstandard dialect. One major source of confusion has been to identify nonstandard dialect with restricted code. Bernstein himself is quite clear that these are quite distinct concepts, and that one can have elaborated and restricted variants of both standard and nonstandard English:

> There is nothing, but nothing, in the dialect [of nonstandard speakers] as such which prevents a child from internalizing and learning to use universalistic meanings. (*CCC 1*, p. 224)

(One might add, however, that Bernstein himself is partly to blame for this confusion, since his rare examples of restricted code have often been in nonstandard dialect.)

3.6 Conclusions

Bernstein's work is widely taught on courses in education and sociology, and is accepted as established fact by many people, but his theories have now attracted a considerable amount of fundamental criticism. Among the most critical reviews, the reader is referred to: Labov (1969), who argues that no detailed specification has been given of the central concept of code, and that the experimental results are artefacts of the experimental situations; Rosen (1973), who questions Bernstein's concept of social class and the lack of linguistic data; Jackson (1974), who argues that Bernstein's work 'fails by rather obvious intellectual tests' in that the theory is untestable and unrelated to linguistic evidence; Trudgill (1975b, quoted above), who questions the lack of linguistic exemplification and argues that the language differences Bernstein found are simply differences in style; and Gordon who calls the work 'pseudo-theory' and 'fundamentally unscientific' (1981, p. 73). Bernstein replies to some of his critics in the introduction and postscript to *CCC 1* (1973), and the introduction by Halliday to *CCC 2* is a statement by a linguist more sympathetic to Bernstein's argument. There is clearly still room for debate (see Ch. 4.4).

For alternative reviews of this area, readers are referred to: Dittmar (1976), who provides a Marxist critique of Bernstein's work (and also Labov's, see Ch. 4) and an annotated comprehensive bibliography of work up to 1976 on the concept of verbal deprivation; J. R. Edwards (1979), who provides further references up to 1979; Stubbs (1980, Ch. 7), who provides a slightly broader critique of the debate over verbal deficit than is given here; and Gordon (1981), who provides an excellent brief summary of Bernstein's work and makes explicit some assumptions underlying verbal deficit theory.

No critic of Bernstein's has ever denied that there *are* social-class differences in language, or that these differences are *somehow* related to educational problems faced by WC children. What is in dispute is the nature of the relationship. MC children tend to score higher than WC ones in tests of academic ability;

and MC language is likely to be closer to the standard language. Both these propositions may be true, but it remains to be demonstrated that they are causally related.

The main point of my own discussion of Bernstein's work has been to urge extreme caution in interpreting the findings (which are extremely interesting in themselves) of social-class differences in language use. It is not clear that the work provides any explanation for these differences, and alternative explanations are still open. Their importance might lie, for example, in people's *attitudes* to such differences, rather than in the differences themselves (see Ch. 2.1).

Often Bernstein's work has been taken simply as further evidence of inequalities in the education system. This is unfair, and treats the work at a trivial theoretical level. Atkinson (1981) provides a detailed argument that Bernstein's work is to be interpreted as a contribution to the tradition of European structuralist sociology, and that his work on sociolinguistic codes is only one part of this. But theories have to explain data, and if the data do not fit, then it is the theory which has to be altered or abandoned. It seems, therefore, that Bernstein's theories will remain uncorroborated until they can be formulated in such a way that they can be closely related to linguistic data collected by observation and recording in homes and classrooms. Chapter 8 will suggest how some of Bernstein's concepts can be related to observations inside classrooms, and will discuss how his later work seeks also to show how social class acts on the distribution of knowledge in society and thereby relates to social power and control.

At present, however, the naturalistic data which are available from other sources only adds to the difficulty in interpreting Bernstein's abstract model. This is the topic of the next chapter.

4

Labov and the myth of linguistic deprivation

William Labov is Professor of Linguistics at the University of Pennsylvania, USA. Since the mid-1960s, he has revolutionized the study of sociolinguistics. He has published important work on the way a speaker's language reflects his or her social class, and descriptions of varieties of nonstandard English used by different ethnic groups in the USA, for example Blacks and Puerto Ricans in New York. Many of his papers are on technical aspects of sociolinguistics and language change, but he has also written many influential articles on language in education, including articles on the relationship between reading problems and nonstandard English and peer-group membership, and oral story-telling styles. Several of his articles on educational topics are collected in Labov (1972a), and other theoretical papers on language and social class are collected in Labov (1972b). A great deal of work has been published in both the USA and Britain to develop Labov's work on the relation between varieties of English and educational problems. Outstanding contributions include Macaulay (1978) on language and education in Glasgow; Milroy (1980) on nonstandard English in WC areas of Belfast;

and V. K. Edwards (1979) and Sutcliffe (1981) on British Black English.

Labov's work gains its power from two sources. First, it is based on long-term, intensive *fieldwork* and *participant observation* in the speech communities he has investigated. Characteristically, Labov has tape-recorded speakers, not only in interviews, but in situations which were as natural as possible. To study the language of Black adolescents in the urban ghettoes of New York, for example, he spent time getting to know his informants, used a Black colleague as one of the investigators, and observed and recorded his informants in their usual surroundings in Harlem, in the gangs with which they spent their time. Second, his arguments are based closely on detailed analyses of the actual language recorded: not on surface analyses of a few dialect features, but on analyses of nonstandard dialects in depth, as self-consistent language systems. Labov's work is therefore important for its linguistically detailed analyses of *spontaneous language* collected as far as possible in its *natural social context of use*.

One of Labov's most important papers is 'The logic of nonstandard English' (1969). If I had to recommend one single paper to readers of this book it would be this one, and a summary of the main linguistic concepts in this paper provides a good introduction to an approach to language in education which is very different to the approach we saw in Chapter 3. The central concern of the article is to show that the concept of *verbal deprivation* is a myth, unsupported by linguistic and anthropological evidence. To show this, Labov discusses the misunderstandings which are possible about the relationships between language, concept formation, explicitness and logic.

4.1 Languages, logic, explicitness and grammar

Labov points out a first possible confusion between logic and explicitness. A criticism often raised against pupils' speech by teachers is that it is 'badly connected' and inexplicit. Teachers

68

often feel this about Black English Vernacular (BEV) which has sentences like: 'he my brother' (SE: 'he's my brother'). But there are many languages which do not use the verb *to be* in such sentences, for example Russian: 'on moj brat' (literally: 'he my brother'). Other languages which use no verbal connective in such sentences include Hungarian and Arabic. Such languages may be foreign, but they are not inexplicit because the verb *to be* is not used in certain types of sentences. Further, it would be ludicrous to argue that a Russian had a defective concept of existential relationships, just because of this detail in the grammar of his language. One must therefore be quite clear that if we teach children to insert connectives and use standard syntax in such sentences, then we are only teaching them slightly different forms of surface grammar. We are neither developing their logic or concepts, nor teaching them to be explicit.

A comparable example occurs with BEV forms like: 'He come yesterday' (SE: 'he came yesterday'). Failure to mark explicitly the past tense in the verb does not indicate a failure to perceive past time. It merely means that in BEV *come* is in the same class as verbs like *put* and *hit* in SE (cf. 'I always *put* it there, I *put* it there yesterday').

It is also easy to confuse logic and grammar. Many nonstandard dialects of British and American English use double or multiple negatives such as: 'I don't know nothing' (SE: 'I don't know anything'). It is sometimes said that such sentences are illogical on the grounds that if I *don't* know *nothing*, then I *do* know *something*. One might call this the pseudo-algebraic view of language: two negatives make a positive. (Proponents of this view never explain why the two negatives might not add together to make a stronger negative!) And again, many languages use double negatives (e.g. French: 'je N'en sais RIEN'. Spanish: 'yo NO sé NADA'). Again, these languages may be foreign, but they are not illogical just because they often use two participles to negativize a sentence. And within such languages, including BEV, the use of such double negatives is regular and rule-governed.

We must be careful, then, not to confuse logic, grammar and

explicitness, or to confuse the conventions of SE grammar with universal canons of logic and thought.

The complexity of grammatical rules

In general, Labov points out that we have almost no knowledge of the cognitive correlates of grammar. One reason for this is that the grammatical system which a normal native speaker of any dialect or language commands is much more complex than most people realize, and much more complex than the type of conceptual operation typically tested in 'intelligence tests'. Labov gives the following example.

All speakers of any dialect of English can correctly use words such as *any*, *one* and *ever*, although the rules governing them are highly complex. One cannot, for example, use *anyone* in sentences with a simple past or progressive tense. That is, one cannot say: 'Anyone went to the party' or 'Anyone is going to the party'. These constraints mean that speakers know unconsciously that *anyone* has a feature (+ hypothetical), since it *is* possible to say: '*If* anyone went to the party, . . .'

Another complex and abstract property of *anyone* is that it has a feature (+ distributive). That is, if we want just one more player for a game, we can say to a group of people: 'Do any of you want to play?' We do not, in this case, say: 'Do some of you want to play?' With *any* we are considering a group as individuals, that is, distributively.

The importance of such analyses of the details of language is that they reveal the cognitive complexity involved in *any* speaker's use of language. In particular, it becomes absurd to accuse any dialect of any language of being logically deficient, when any dialect is based on many hundreds of such rules involving such abstract underlying concepts and principles.

Nonstandard dialects as consistent linguistic systems

Speakers of a standard language often interpret grammatical deviations from the standard as random 'errors' due to 'ignorance', 'carelessness' or 'slovenly' speech. Labov exposes this faulty equation of linguistic competence with SE. It is all too easy to assume that if someone's language is *different* from SE, then it is *deficient*. But there is no linguistic evidence for equating such differences with deficit. The work of Labov and others in the Black speech communities of the inner city areas in the USA has documented in detail that BEV is a coherent, systematic, highly structured, rule-governed linguistic system. The notion that the language of socially improverished groups is 'deficient' or structurally underdeveloped rests on a serious misunderstanding of the nature of human language (cf. Ch. 2.2). In fact, BEV is very closely related to SE with which it shares the bulk of its grammatical and lexical systems. And the differences between the two language varieties are systematic, not random. All the evidence demonstrates that when any child (unless severely mentally retarded) comes to school at the age of 5, he has control of a complex linguistic system, so complex in fact that linguists are not yet able to describe it fully.

Teachers may often overestimate the differences between their pupils' nonstandard language and SE. In a study of Glasgow speech (which replicates some of Labov's work in New York), Macaulay (1978) found that many teachers believed that their WC pupils spoke 'two languages': 'English' in the classroom and 'Glaswegian' elsewhere. But the children could not be held to speak two languages under any reasonable definition of 'language'. There is not even any evidence of a Glasgow dialect, distinct from other varieties of English. At most children shift in *style* inside and outside the classroom, and these style-shifts are mainly in pronunciation, with a few superficial grammatical and lexical differences. Pronunciation or accent is, of course, literally the most superficial and easily observable aspect of language, and often attracts more attention than it merits. (Consider again in this connection the debate over whether Bernstein has put his finger on fundamental differences in 'code' or has merely documented stylistic differences between WC and MC speakers. See Ch. 3.4.)

71

4.2 Nonstandard languages as media of education

When it is realized that nonstandard languages and dialects are highly complex, coherent language systems, based on many hundreds of abstract patterns and regularities, it must also be admitted that there is no *linguistic* reason why such language varieties should not be the media of instruction in schools. It is believed in many speech communities that nonstandard dialects are fit only for non-serious purposes (such as casual conversation, telling anecdotes, joking) but are not suited to discussion of intellectually demanding topics. Teachers have been known to assert that 'There are things that you can't say' in such-and-such a dialect, implying that the dialect is deficient in vocabulary. But the vocabulary of English is a resource available to all its dialects: any word can be used in any nonstandard utterance. Characteristically, there are stylistic constraints on the co-occurrence of items, so that sentences such as: 'Them linguists don't know nothing about morphophonemics' sound odd. But such stylistic conventions cannot constitute a constraint on the speaker's thinking. There is no evidence, then, that any non-standard language variety is, *in itself*, an unsuitable medium for education and intellectual discussion.

Strong, independent confirmation of this comes from work on *pidgin* and *creole* languages (see Hall, 1972). Pidgins are languages which develop as simplified versions of a source language (such as English, French and Portuguese) in restricted situations in which speakers of the source language have to communicate with a native population. Thus, Melanesian Pidgin English developed from English, and pidgins in Haiti, Martinique, Guadeloupe and Mauritius developed from French. Such pidgins are much simpler in grammar and lexis than their source language, irregularities being reduced or eliminated. And functionally a pidgin is much simpler than its source, being used only as a lingua franca in limited trading situations, and by definition not being a native language of any of those who speak it. But although structurally simpler than 'normal' languages, pidgins are still real languages, governed by complex rules which are difficult to learn. (The commonsense meaning of 'pidgin English' as a crude communication system with no proper grammar and only a few dozen words is *very* misleading.) A creole is a pidgin which has then become the native language of a group of people. Structurally (or linguistically) it may be identical to the pidgin from which it developed. But functionally it now serves a group in all their everyday communication, and is learned by children as their native language.

Despite their relative structural simplicity, pidgins and creoles are quite satisfactory media for conveying complex technological information, and manuals in fields such as medicine have been prepared in them. The belief of policy makers that such languages are not suitable as media of instruction is not therefore supported by the linguistic evidence. Creoles are perfectly satisfactory media of communication in schools. Indeed, it is only sensible in many cases to make children literate initially in the only language they know (Stubbs, 1980).

Note, however, that the local population themselves, who speak a creole as their native language, may hold the creole in such low esteem that they do not wish their children to be taught in it. It is a finding of sociolinguistic studies in different parts of the world that speakers of social groups who are low in prestige relative to another social group tend to downgrade their *own* ethnic-linguistic group. Thus *both* English Canadians and French Canadians regard Canadian French speakers less favourably than English speakers, both groups sharing the community-wide stereotype of French Canadians as relatively second-rate people (Lambert, 1967). And speakers of BEV (Mitchell-Kernan, 1972) and of Glaswegian English (Macaulay, 1978) have very ambivalent attitudes towards their own language. Although it symbolizes group loyalty for them, they tend to regard prestige SE as 'better'. As always in the sociolinguistics of language in education, speakers' attitudes are crucial.

4.3 The myth of linguistic deprivation

One reason for supposing that Negro children from the ghetto areas have deficient language has been the assumption that they do not receive enough 'verbal stimulation' in the home. But Labov has shown that this too is false, and that Negro children typically hear *more* well-formed sentences than MC children and participate in a highly verbal culture. The high value placed on verbal skills in Afro-American culture is now well documented by field studies (e.g. Labov, 1972a; Kochman, 1972). Expertise in speech is much more highly valued than in MC culture (which places a high value on written language) and the Black community has a rich oral tradition quite alien to Whites.

Experiments on language 'deprivation'

If direct observation of Black speech communities immediately dispels notions of 'linguistic deprivation', where do such notions come from? One source is artificial experiments with mothers and children. In a much quoted study, Hess and Shipman (1965) investigated how 163 Negro mothers from different social-class backgrounds set about teaching their 4 year old children tasks, such as sorting toys by colour and function. They found differences in the teaching strategies of mothers in different social-class groups, and claim that such data provide evidence of 'cultural deprivation' in lower social-class groups which 'depresses the resources of the human mind', due to a 'lack of cognitive meaning in the mother–child communication system'. I have argued above that such concepts are not supported by linguistic or anthropological evidence, so what evidence do Hess and Shipman provide, and why do I find it unconvincing?

Hess and Shipman found that after the teaching sessions the MC children had learned the tasks better than the WC children, and they attempt to explain this by reference to the mothers' language. They found that the MC mothers talked more to their children, used more abstract words, and more syntactically complex language. They claim that these differences reveal a 'deprivation of meaning' in the WC mother–child relationship. But as we have seen already (Ch. 3.4), such comparisons cannot demonstrate that a group of speakers is 'deprived' of anything. The WC mothers *did* talk to their children, *did* use abstract words, and *did* use syntactically complex language. (In fact, the differences quoted between the highest and lowest status groups are not very large. For example, mean sentence length was 11·4 words for the college educated group and 8·2 words for the WC group from an unskilled occupational level with fathers absent and on public assistance. No levels of statistical significance are quoted, which makes such figures impossible to interpret.) Therefore, the experiment shows that WC mothers *do* have access to the meanings which can be conveyed by such linguistic resources – they are not 'deprived of meanings' at all. In the experimental situation, WC mothers apparently chose not to express such meanings quite as often as MC mothers, but that is quite a different matter.

In fact, the statistical linguistic analysis appears to bear no relation to the mother–child dialogues which were the data. Hess and Shipman quote some extracts from these dialogues. One mother explained a task to her child as follows:

> All right. Susan, this board is the place where we put the little toys; first of all you're supposed to learn how to place them according to colour. Can you do that? The things that are all the same colour you put in one section . . .

Another mother was much less explicit:

> M: I've got some chairs and cars, do you want to play the game? OK, what's this?
> C: A wagon?
> M: Hm?
> C: A wagon?
> M: This is not a wagon. What's this?

Clearly, the second teaching style is less adequate than the first. And I imagine that the difference in educational effect of the two

75

mothers' teaching styles is considerable, if this is indeed how these children are regularly spoken to. But the inadequacy has nothing to do with average sentence length or the number of complex sentences! The second mother simply does not explain what the child should do. What does require explanation is why WC mothers, in this situation, are not motivated to explain things in sufficient detail in their children. The superficial analysis of language form which Hess and Shipman provide is largely irrelevant to this question.

As always with experiments in laboratory settings, there is also the criticism that the highest status group (defined here as college educated) were simply more at home in the test situation. All the mothers were brought to the university for testing, although only the college educated group would ever have been inside such an institution before. The differences in WC and MC teaching strategies might be an artefact of the test situation itself. Certainly, the tests were heavily *culture biased* in favour of the MC mothers and children, since they involved playing with the kind of toys much more likely to be found in MC homes. Always in work of this kind we come up against the danger of interpreting speakers' use of language in a strange or threatening context (a 'test') while doing unfamiliar tasks, as their total verbal capacity. We must always be particularly critical of the sources of data in such experiments, and ask whether the apparent linguistic incompetence of certain social groups is not in fact *generated by the research itself*. Such research, in other words, fails to take into account that the social situation of the research itself is likely to be a crucial determinant of data (see Ch. 5.3).

The social context as determinant of language use

A major finding of sociolinguistics is that the *social context* is the most powerful determinant of verbal behaviour. Fieldwork with Black children (e.g. Labov, 1969) has shown that they produce vivid, complex language in unstructured situations with friends, but may appear monosyllabic and defensive in asymmetrical classroom or test situations where an adult has power over them. Philips (1972) has found exactly the same with American Indian children: that they are expressive outside the classroom, but silent, reticent and defensive inside it with their White teachers (see Ch. 7.5).

The very notion of 'testing' someone by asking him questions to which there are correct verbal answers is a strongly culture-bound notion not shared by many social groups. Thus the type of behaviour found by Hess and Shipman may merely represent the different sociolinguistic constraints which control language in different social groups. Certainly there is little connection between the kind of language demanded by such 'tests' and the kind of language valued by WC Negro culture. So it simply does not make sense to take language used in tests as a measure of total language capacity – and far less as a measure of cognitive capacity. Interview, interrogation, test or classroom situations simply do not tap the verbal ability of such speakers.

It is important to realize also how different social groups may react in widely different ways to what are apparently the 'same' situations. MC Whites take it for granted that teaching and testing involve teachers asking questions and pupils giving answers. But different ethnic groups interpret questioning in radically different ways. Thus WC Blacks may identify questioning with the prying questions of welfare agencies. Some American Indian groups regard direct questions as an unforgivable invasion of personal privacy (Dumont, 1972). Hawaiian children will often talk freely to adults whom they believe to be interested in hearing them, but will refuse to answer direct questions (Boggs, 1972). In other words, different groups have quite different sociolinguistic assumptions about how and when it is appropriate to talk to different audiences.

The social pathology model

What Labov is arguing against is the *social pathology model* of language and intelligence. The social pathology model starts from the undeniable *differences* in language and culture between different social groups, say WC Negroes and MC Whites in the USA, and from the undeniable fact that, compared with Whites, Negro children are unsuccessful at school. It then falsely interprets differences as the cause of failure at school, by falsely interpreting *differences* as *deficits*. The model then characteristically goes on to argue that these deficits are transmitted by the family environment by, for example, inadequate child-rearing practices. The door is then open for the argument that to cure the 'deficits', what is required is interventionist programmes (known also as compensatory, enrichment or Headstart programmes): that is, pre-school programmes designed to improve or enrich the child's supposedly deficient language.

But it is now generally admitted that such interventionist programmes have failed. That is, giving the underprivileged Negro children intensive linguistic training before they start school does not help their school achievement. The reason is simply that such programmes are designed to cure deficits that are not there. The work of Labov and others has shown in detail that Negro children do not have deficient language. So, teaching a child SE in pre-school programmes will only teach him or her slightly different forms of a language he or she already knows.

Labov points out that a major problem for speakers of nonstandard dialects at school is the mutual ignorance of teachers and pupils of each others' language. Teachers have often no systematic knowledge of the nonstandard forms which contrast with SE. And some teachers do not believe that nonstandard dialects *are* systematic although this has been shown in detail. They attribute what is a different, but rule-governed and systematic dialect to 'sloppiness' or 'mistakes'. Such mutual ignorance is not surprising since few people have the opportunity of hearing a wide range of speakers in a wide range of social situations. A teacher's evaluation of a pupil's language is typically made on the basis of his or her restricted response to a hostile classroom or test situation. Whereas a true picture of a child's verbal capacity could only come from studying his or her language across the range of social situations in which it developed.

4.4 Labov and Bernstein

It is part of the myth about linguistic deprivation to believe that Labov has produced a definitive refutation of Bernstein's theories. As an American researcher has expressed it to me: 'The idea is widespread in the USA that Labov has discredited Bernstein and the strong implication is made that if you don't agree with that, you're a racist.' There is also confusion over this in Britain. For example, Tough asserts that 'there have been many criticisms of Bernstein's work, most notably by William Labov' (1977, p. 31). This is inaccurate.

Labov and Bernstein have commented only very briefly on each other's work. Labov (1969, 1970) accuses Bernstein of failing to provide a proper linguistic specification of the central concept of code, and of failing to relate the theory to actual data on the use of language in context. He also believes that what Bernstein treats as code differences are merely stylistic preferences between speakers. Bernstein (CCC 3, p. 28) accuses much of the American work on sociolinguistics of being conducted at a trivial theoretical level, in so far as it is not related to wider problems of the socialization of the child, cultural transmission and change. He accuses the American work on BEV (including, presumably, Labov's) of being limited to relatively surface concepts of 'context' and 'language variety', and of neglecting to analyse the deeper, underlying problems of how educational knowledge is transmitted. Both sides of the debate are, it seems to me, making valid points. It is a pity that there has so far been no detailed discussion of the issues by those directly involved in the debate. It would be illuminating for all of us.

It is clear that much of Labov's work implicitly questions Bernstein's theory. But direct comparison is difficult. Bernstein's work is experimental and/or abstract and speculative, rather than being based on details of observed language in use. Labov's most important work, on the other hand, is closely based on detailed linguistic analyses of language recorded during fieldwork in natural social situations. It is also not clear how far observations of the language of WC Negroes in the USA can be extrapolated to a British context.

4.5 West Indian children in British Schools

Very important work has, however, been done in Britain with West Indian children aged seven to nine in city schools, and this British work confirms several principles which have emerged from Labov's work in the USA. This work started as a Schools Council Project at the University of Birmingham in 1967 (Wight and Norris, 1970; Wight, 1971, 1975; Sinclair, 1973).

There is considerable variation in the language of West Indian children in Britain, depending on their social class, on which part of the West Indies they come from, and on whether they are recent immigrants or were British-born. Several different terms are used for such varieties. One term is 'Jamaican Creole', and although Jamaicans in Britain are high in numbers, there are different varieties used in other Caribbean islands. 'West Indian English' is another term, although the term 'West Indies' is not normally used by the speakers themselves. They often refer to their language as 'Patois', although this can also refer to French-based creoles (for example, from St Lucia). A neutral term might be 'Caribbean Creoles'. Le Page (1981) and Sutcliffe (1981) provide succinct descriptions of the varieties involved.

At the risk of over-generalization, the home language of many of the children is an English-based creole (see Ch. 4.2) which can be regarded as an extreme dialect of English. That is, creole and SE lie at opposite ends of a dialect continuum whose extremes are mutually unintelligible language varieties. The differences between the language variety spoken in the home and the SE used in schools can cause educational problems for such children, but only indirectly. In the infant school, some creole-speaking children may initially be unintelligible to the teacher. But by the age of 5, most children are bidialectal in creole and a classroom dialect which approximates to SE. And by the age of

7, most children have an impressive command of SE. Interference from creole is not therefore found to be a major source of children's comprehension problems. Nor does the child's language often impede spoken communication.

The project concluded that the children did not need much remedial English teaching at all, since they acquire the school dialect of their own accord with speed and skill. It was decided that all they require is direct teaching of a few linguistic features necessary to the conventions of standard *written* English. Creole, for example, does not use inflexions in forms like *he come*. Such differences produce no problems in spoken communication, but teaching is needed to bring the children's *writing* into line with conventional usage.

The most important sociolinguistic factor in the education of West Indian children is therefore the *attitude* of the teacher. It is crucial, for example, that initial minor difficulties in comprehension are correctly attributed to dialect interference and not to lack of intelligence. The main requirement here is patience and tolerance of dialect differences on the part of the teacher.

The most interesting discovery was that the problems in language development which many of the children have are not due to dialect differences at all, but are shared by numerous children whose native dialect is SE. And language materials which were originally developed for West Indian children have been found to be useful for all children. These materials, published by E. J. Arnold as *Concept 7–9*, aim at developing language effectiveness and communication competence, rather than spending time on superficial features of dialect, which were found to be scarcely educationally relevant. Wight (1975) points out that a central theoretical weakness in the language deprivation concept is that it is derived from an *un*defined notion of language proficiency: it is such proficiency that the materials aim to develop. The *Concept 7–9* materials are in the form of a beautifully produced package of games, designed mainly to be played between the children themselves. One game among many, for example, provides one child with different shapes drawn on cards, say:

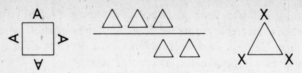

The child has to describe the shapes to his or her partner who has to draw them working only from the verbal description, not being allowed to see the original. This game can be made quite difficult: readers might try describing this shape so that some-one else could draw it *exactly* , maintaining the same shape and size of the spirals and numeral forms.

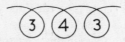

The main strategy of the games is thus to get the children talking to each other within well-defined communication tasks. And the idea of the games is to force the children to explain, describe, inquire, classify and differentiate, as accurately as is required for the game. As Sinclair says:

> It is fascinating to watch children using the communication materials. They are so intent on solving the problem that they squeeze their language to the last drop of meaning, flash from one tactic to another, try new angles with all sorts of risks involved. (1973)

The work therefore confirms the general finding quoted above (see Chs. 3.2, 4.3) that measures of a child's linguistic competence in a potentially threatening or embarrassing adult–child situation are simply no measure of his or her true capacity. A major feature of the *Concept 7–9* materials is that many of the games are designed to be played between children with no adult intervening, after an initial explanation of the rules. The project and subsequent work have produced large amounts of materials for use in schools.

V. K. Edwards's (1979) work does, however, suggest some modifications to Wight's position. Edwards argues that there are some differences between standard British English and

Caribbean creoles which may cause interference problems between the dialects, and therefore comprehension problems for children in reading. She gives many such examples. One is that Caribbean creoles do not necessarily distinguish between active and passive sentences. For example, a sentence such as *The chickens eat* might be ambiguous to a child who might interpret it as either 'The chickens eat' or as 'The chickens are eaten'. Nevertheless, she also emphasizes the range of other non-linguistic factors which may contribute to educational problems: the children and their parents may have different educational expectations from White MC British people, they may be under severe social and economic pressures, and, as always, the teachers' attitudes are crucial.

In a revised version of his earlier articles, Wight (1979) still maintains that children of Caribbean origin do not find learning to read more difficult because of differences between their home dialect and SE. The important factor, he maintains, is the teachers' attitude to such differences. The debate is therefore not yet resolved.

Wight (1979) also points out that the dialect situation for children of Caribbean origin may be more complex than that I described in Chapter 2.3. For example, a child in London may have two different prestige standard varieties of English to aim at in formal situations, as well as a British nonstandard dialect and distinct varieties of Caribbean creole and London Jamaican (now distinct from Jamaican Creole) to move towards in less formal situations. According to the social setting, he or she will move in a stylistic and dialectal space defined by at least five norms:

Standard	*Nonstandard*
Standard British English	Nonstandard London dialect
Standard Jamaican English	London Jamaican
	Caribbean Creole

The Rampton Report on West Indian children in British schools has asserted that 'schools should value the language which all children, including West Indians, bring to school'

(HMSO, 1981). Since the Bullock Report (HMSO, 1975) this has become almost an official litany. However, it is probably much more often asserted than put into practice or even understood. I have already shown in this book that to understand what is meant requires an understanding of the complex relations between informal spoken language, nonstandard dialects and the standard language expected in formal educational settings.

4.6 A pseudo-problem?

The large, complex and imposing literature on the importance of language in education (the present book being a very small drop in a rather rough ocean) must not blind us to simple *non*linguistic reasons why WC (and immigrant) children tend to fail at school more often than MC children. For example, a child may fail at school because he does not share the school's ideas of what is important: he just has different values and commitments. One nonlinguistic explanation of failure at school is that you can take a child to Euclid but you can't make him think. Alternatively, a child may appear 'uneducable' because the school is insensitive to his culturally different forms of language and thinking, and insists on treating such differences as deficits. A second explanation of educational failure is that you have to start teaching from where the child is: there is nowhere else to start – but with different children we have to start in different places. Nor must we assume in any case that there has to be a *single*, tidy cause of educational failure: a single, magic predictor of educational progress. In general, there is increasing evidence for a range of nontraditional (including nonlinguistic) effects on cognitive development, including the child's confidence in himself and hopes for the future, and the teacher's expectations of him or her (Rosenthal and Jacobson, 1968).

The reader is warned, therefore, not to be taken in by the large number of studies which discuss whether there is a *direct causal* relationship between language and educability. Large amounts of academic ink have often been wasted on pseudo-problems. In the Middle Ages, scholars used to debate how many angels could dance on the point of a needle: but debating a problem does not make it meaningful in real world terms. Several widely read books (e.g. Creber, 1972; Wilkinson, 1971; Flower, 1966; Herriot, 1971) on language in education simply take for granted that 'linguistic deprivation' is a meaningful concept, and that it can be used to 'explain' some children's educational problems. The concept, however, is severely in dispute, and many linguists question whether the notion has any validity whatsoever. In fact, a counter literature has now sprung up out of necessity to point out some of the myths created by social-science research in education. Keddie (1973) attacks the 'myth' of cultural deprivation; Labov (1969) attacks one aspect of this myth in what he calls the 'illusion of verbal deprivation'; and Jackson (1974) attacks the 'myth' of elaborated and restricted codes. It is unfortunate that one group of social scientists is now having to try and clear up some of the confusion caused by another group: unfortunate but necessary, since these are not mere debates between academics, but live issues affecting teachers and their pupils.

The general message of the last two chapters, then, is that a great deal of the literature on the relation between language and educational success is rather beside the point. There is, as yet, no proven *causal* relationship between a child's language and his cognitive ability, and it is not even clear what kind of evidence would be required to demonstrate such a relationship. Statements which assert that certain (dialectal) varieties of language are 'deficient', and therefore *cause* cognitive deficiencies, are demonstrably incoherent. A major logical fallacy derives therefore from seeing language as a cause of educational success or failure. Since no clearcut relation can be demonstrated between forms of language and forms of cognition, one is left with a mere *correlation*: two groups of children, say WC and MC, use different varieties of language and also (as a statistical tendency) perform differently at school. But such a *correlation* can never, in itself, be a demonstration of *causality*.

A sociolinguistic problem

What emerges, however, is a complex sociolinguistic relationship between a child's language and his success at school. There is no doubt that different social groups *use* different forms of language in comparable social situations. That is, they have different norms of appropriate language use. This is shown both by fieldwork in natural settings, and also by experimental work such as Bernstein's. Teachers and schools may find the language used by certain children stylistically inappropriate to the conventions of the classroom situation; although the child's language may be quite adequate to any cognitive demands made on it. Further, teachers may react negatively to low-prestige varieties of language, and, in extreme situations, may even misunderstand the child (although neither party may realize precisely what is happening). Even if the teacher goes out of his way to accept the child's language as different but equally valuable, his own language is likely to be noticeably different from the child's in the direction of the standard, prestige language variety. And the child will be aware that the teacher's form of language is the one supported by institutional authority. Children may then be caught in a double bind. They may recognize that to get ahead they must adopt the teacher's style of language, but to do this will separate them from their friends. A nonstandard dialect may have low social prestige for schools, but serve the positive functions of displaying group loyalty for its speakers. And the peer group is always a much stronger linguistic influence on children than either school or family. Statements about language in education must always take into account, therefore, the power of speakers' attitudes, beliefs and perceptions of language. There is almost no one in Britain who is not now constantly exposed to models of SE through education, radio, television and the press. But there is no evidence that local speech varieties are dying. Pressures to conformity are always offset by pressures of loyalty to the local speech community. This is as true of speakers of nonstandard Negro English as of Glaswegians (Macaulay, 1978).

Educational *disadvantage* may be the result of people's ignorance or intolerance of cultural and linguistic *differences*. But such a disadvantage is not a *deficit*. I would thus reject the over-simple and dangerous catchphrase 'educational failure is linguistic failure', and substitute for it the more guarded statement: 'Educational failure often results from sociolinguistic differences between schools and pupils.' My own view is therefore as follows: (1) schools and classrooms depend on language, since education, as we understand it in our culture, is inconceivable without the lecturing, explaining, reading and writing which comprise it (see Chs. 1.2 and 7.5). So, (2) if a school defines a pupil as 'linguistically inadequate' then he or she will almost certainly fail in the formal educational system. But this a tautology: (2) follows directly from (1), and merely raises the question of what linguistic demands schools make on pupils. One of the linguistic demands made by the school may be that SE is the appropriate language for the classroom. If linguistic competence is thus equated with the ability to use standard dialect forms, this means that speakers of nonstandard dialects are by definition 'linguistically deficient'. But such a definition is, of course, a circular and empty one, and has no basis whatsoever in linguistic fact.

Since I am arguing that sociolinguistic breakdown often occurs between pupils and schools, the rest of this book must look at ways of studying the language used by teachers and pupils in classrooms.

5

The need for studies of classroom language

We are now half-way through this book without having discussed directly how teachers and pupils use language in actual, everyday classroom situations. This is a sad reflection on the state of our knowledge about language in education, and on the failure of most researchers, until recently, to go where the action is: into classrooms.

5.1 Reasons for studying classroom language

There are important reasons for observing, recording and studying teacher–pupil dialogue in the classroom.

The most fundamental reason is that, ultimately, the classroom dialogue between teachers and pupils *is* the educational process, or, at least, the major part of it for most children. Other factors, such as children's language, IQ, social class and home background, however important they may be as contributing factors, are nevertheless external, background influences. Relatively little educational research, paradoxical as this may seem, has been based on direct observation and recording of the teaching process, as it happens, in the classroom itself. There was for a long time an assumption that the educational process could be explained by looking at the *external determinants* of educational success and failure, and outcomes (as measured by tests and questionnaires), but without looking *inside* classrooms. On commonsense grounds alone, however, it would seem that an understanding of teaching and learning would have to depend, at least in part, on observation of teachers and learners. There is an enormous psychological literature on 'learning theory' based largely on experimental situations, but very little is known about what and how children learn in schools. The only way to discover this is to observe children in classrooms.

It was emphasized above, for example, that in Bernstein's work, although much of it is concerned with educability, no attempt is made to examine how language is used in schools. Bernstein's model proposes external determinants of educational success: social-class stratification is said to produce different family types with different communication systems, which in turn produce different codes and different cognitive orientations in children. He simply states, without evidence or illustrations, that schools are predicated upon elaborated code, since schools are concerned with 'making explicit and elaborating through language, principles and operations' (*CCC 1*, p. 221) and that 'the introduction of the child to the universalistic meanings of public forms of thought . . . *is education*' (*CCC 1*, p. 225, emphasis in original). It will become clear below, in studying actual fragments of transcribed classroom lessons, that classroom language is often highly constrained in some obvious ways, rather than 'elaborated'.

It is also important to realize that these external, background factors are inaccessible and highly interpretive abstractions resting, at least in part, on social interaction. Consider, for example, the concept of a child's IQ. This is not an absolute, pure measure: it is a capacity which has to be measured *in a social situation*, in the classroom or in a test, in which tester *interacts with* pupil. It is now realized in general that learning is not a purely cognitive or psychological process, but can depend crucially on the social relationship between teacher and pupil (see Chs 6.4 and 7.4). In exactly the same way, home background is partly physical environment (e.g. the number of people to a room, or the number of books in the house), but it is also quite inseparable from the *social interaction* in the family (e.g. whether parents discuss homework with the children).

It is important, then, if our statements about education are not to be vague, ungrounded generalizations, to tie these statements down to analyses of actual, observable and recorded talk and communication. It is all too easy to make generalizations about 'classroom atmosphere' which are unrelated to what actually happens in classrooms. I can illustrate this most easily from a quote. Postman and Weingartner discuss how it is that pupils get the message that the language used in school does not have to satisfy the demands of a problem so much as the demands of the teacher, although few teachers consciously articulate such a message as part of the content of their lessons:

> The message is communicated quietly, insidiously, relentlessly and effectively through the structure of the classroom: through the role of the teacher, the role of the student, the rules of their verbal game. . . . Each of these learnings (i.e. what is communicated by the structure of the classroom) is expressed in specific behaviours that are on constant display throughout the culture. (1969, pp. 32–3)

I tend to agree with Postman and Weingartner, but I would want to be much more specific. Given that many messages are conveyed by teachers to pupils, just *how* are they communicated? By *what* 'structure'? What *are* the rules of the verbal game? What specific behaviours? If they are specific, then they can be specified.

5.2 Our ignorance of classroom language

Our ignorance of what actually happens inside classrooms is spectacular. We are often prepared to make broad generalizations purporting to relate children's language to their potential

90

educability, yet we lack basic descriptive information about how pupils and teachers communicate. In a sense, of course, we all know what classrooms are like: we have spent long enough in them as pupils and teachers. But such intuitive, remembered knowledge is no substitute for a conceptually adequate analysis of classroom life based on recording and description of the classroom routine which takes up thousands of hours of a pupil's life. People often hold firmly entrenched views on the language and education debate, often arguing more from prejudice than from carefully considered observations and evidence. In any case, a major problem in studying classroom behaviour is that it takes a tremendous effort to really see what *is* happening: rather than simply taking the scene for granted and interpreting it in terms of conventional categories.

The teaching process has not yet been adequately described in sociolinguistic terms. If one talks to teachers about their classroom experiences, one discovers immediately that there is simply no vocabulary of descriptive concepts for talking about teaching. Despite the vast complexity of second-by-second classroom dialogue, the discussion will be conceptually crude and oversimplified. It is time that teachers had an adequate descriptive language for talking about their own professional behaviour.

The need for sociolinguistic study of classroom language

Sociolinguistic study of teacher–pupil dialogue, observed and recorded in the classroom, would therefore begin to fill a serious gap left by previous research on language in education.

The assumption that all the important determinants of classroom performance lie outside the classroom is no longer so widely held, and classroom research is developing fast. However, most research which has been based on direct observation of teacher–pupil interaction in the classroom has been done exclusively according to techniques of *systematic observation*. In using techniques of this type, an observer sits in the classroom and uses a set of pre-prepared categories to 'code' what teachers and pupils say, usually every few seconds on a time-sampling basis. Coding categories might include, for example, 'teacher lectures', 'pupil asks question' and 'teacher justifies authority'. Over seventy coding schemes have been published (Simon and Boyer, 1967, 1970) and literally hundreds of studies have been done with such systems. But results for research have been disappointing, and no clear trends have emerged, for example, between teachers' verbal styles, as defined by the schemes, and measures of teaching effectiveness. This type of work is covered by several comprehensive reviews (e.g. Medley and Mitzel, 1963). More recent articles have thoroughly documented reasons for disillusionment with the technique as a research tool, though not necessarily as a teacher-training method (Nuthall, 1968; Walker and Adelman, 1975b; Delamont, 1983).

The most important shortcomings of this type of study, very briefly, are as follows. Since the classroom talk is generally not recorded but 'coded' by the observer on the spot in real time, the actual language used by teachers and pupils is irretrievably lost. Such a technique can therefore at best provide an overall, average measure of classroom climate or atmosphere, without being able to study the details of the actual talk which create this climate. In other words, there is no study of how hearers (researchers as well as pupils and teachers) interpret classroom language: it is assumed that the coder can do this unproblematically. Hence, the data for study are not in fact the classroom language at all, but the researcher's codings of it. In general, the technique focuses in a fragmentary way on a succession of small bits of behaviour, through pre-specified categories which allow no adaptation or development. It deals only with what is immediately observable to the researcher, ignoring qualitative factors in favour of what is easily quantifiable (Delamont and Hamilton, 1976).

Given that relatively little analysis has been based on direct observation of classroom behaviour, it would in any case be premature to remain committed to one narrowly defined type of interaction analysis. However, an increasing amount of 'anthropological' or 'ethnographic' research is now being done in

92

schools. Such work itself covers a wide range of styles, as befits its often innovatory and exploratory aims. In general, it is based on long-term or intensive *fieldwork*, that is, on some form of *participant observation*. The researcher may spend several days or weeks actually in the classroom, observing, taking notes, recording, talking to teachers and pupils and getting to know them: the aim being to produce a report resembling an *ethnographic* description of a social setting, similar in some way to the report an anthropologist might write after fieldwork with an exotic tribe! (See Jackson, 1968; Stubbs and Delamont, 1976; Delamont, 1983; and many other references in these works.) Most such studies inevitably discuss aspects of classroom interaction, but they are not centrally concerned to discuss sociolinguistic behaviour.

So there are, as yet, very few studies of classroom life which use sociolinguistic concepts to analyse teacher–pupil talk. This lacuna is odd since sociolinguistics means simply the study of language and how it is used in social settings: such as the classroom. The lacuna results simply but sadly from the lack of communication among experts in different aspects of communication! Social interaction has been studied in fragmentary fashion from within different academic disciplines, including linguistics, anthropology, psychology and sociology. But these disciplines have different methods and aims, and the insulation of these academic areas from each other is almost complete. It should be emphasized, then, that no single approach is widely accepted in studies of classroom language. Different methods are used to do fieldwork, to collect, analyse and present data, according to different underlying objectives.

The tide does now seem to have turned, however, in favour of classroom studies, which have now gained respectability as a legitimate style of research. Various historical factors have contributed to this development since the late 1960s: relatively more money becoming available for educational research; a wider social-psychological model of learning being proposed by educationalists; an increasing emphasis on teacher training; schools becoming more 'open' and therefore easier of access;

93

and the development of appropriate methods of participant observation in sociology (Delamont and Hamilton, 1976).

5.3 The rationale for naturalistic studies

Theoretical reasons are also given, however, for neglecting studies of classroom life, and we have to answer these. It is often argued that studies of real, everyday behaviour are 'unscientific' because real-life settings are vastly complex and contain many uncontrollable factors, and because the same situation never occurs twice and the studies are therefore unreplicable. Only by isolating small bits of behaviour in controlled laboratory settings, so it is argued, can we progress slowly but surely towards the truth.

The short answer to these objections is simple: If we want to know how people behave in classrooms, then we have to observe them in classrooms. If we bring them into the psychological laboratory at the local university, then we may discover how they behave there. But this is unlikely to be of enduring interest!

One might rightly object, of course, that the behaviour of teachers and pupils is unnatural even in the classroom in the presence of an intrusive researcher with notebooks or tape-recorder. However, people forget about the tape-recorders after a relatively short period, say a few hours or a couple of days. And, in any case, many of the things one is interested in observing are simply not under conscious control.

A more powerful defence of naturalistic studies is that the natural social pressure of interacting with a group will often overcome the presence of a tape-recorder. This is particularly true of children recorded in their own friendship groups, in which the pressure of interaction with their peers typically outweighs the presence of an observer, and helps approach the unattainable ideal of recording 'normal' language (Labov, 1972a). Recording speakers *away from* their normal social settings, on the other hand, causes severe problems of interpretation and explanation. This is because there is no way of 'controlling' how people interpret and react to unfamiliar social settings, such as interviews or tests. The crucial point is that the psychological laboratory is *not* a neutral setting in which behaviour can be 'controlled'. It is itself a social setting, comprising perhaps, from a child's point of view, a large, strange adult of high prestige, in unfamiliar surroundings, who is testing the child in some unspecified way (see Chs 3.2 and 4.3). One of the main points of Chapter 4 was that the social situation is the strongest determinant of verbal behaviour. And it is for this reason that I questioned the use of laboratory 'tests' in investigating the verbal ability of children or the nature of mother–child dialogue. Most children are, incidentally, most helpful in such situations and will do their best to do what they think the researcher wants them to do, however odd they may find this. Most children have a remarkably high degree of tolerance for the odd tasks which adults often ask of them!

What we are interested in is how people *interpret* classroom language and attach social meanings and values to it (Hymes, 1972). And one cannot, in principle, 'control' how an adult or child interprets his social environment. One might, for example, ask the same form of question to a hundred people. One might, in the style of some verbal tests, hold up an apple and ask, 'What is this?' But there is no way to control how the hearer interprets the question: Do you really not know that it is an apple? Is it a trick question? Or a riddle? Or is it just a starter question, leading into some more sensible and interesting question?

Such points may seem obvious, but researchers have sometimes taken quite absurd steps to try and 'control' variables in experiments in social behaviour. In one particularly artificial study on how people communicate by gesture and posture, experimental subjects were made to wear cardboard masks 'to keep their minds off their facial expression', since the experimenter did not want to investigate this (Mehrabian, 1968). Clearly, such procedures do not 'control' a variable (in this case, facial expression). On the contrary, they probably made the subjects particularly conscious of their facial expression, quite apart from making them feel silly or embarrassed or restricting

95

their sight! Such experiments make the same mistake as the oriental doctor who had discovered a wonderful medicine which could cure his patients of any illness, but only if they did not think of monkeys while they were drinking it. So he used to warn them most particularly not to think about monkeys – and wondered why the medicine never worked. The trouble is that experimental subjects can never be prevented from thinking and forming interpretations about the experiment. One must therefore always take account of people's expectations of experiments. Psychologists who believe that the behaviour of people and rats is essentially similar are likely to construct experiments for humans in which humans would be hard put to it to display anything other than rat-like behaviour. Psychologists who believe, on the other hand, that human behaviour is essentially different, are likely to set up experiments which demand behaviour which is qualitatively different from running through mazes. People, including experimental subjects, generally do what is expected of them: thus fulfilling the experimenters' expectations.

Since the control over behaviour in laboratory settings is largely spurious (one cannot control how people interpret test instructions, for example) the notion that such experiments are replicable is seriously weakened. A powerful form of replicability is, however, possible for studies which attempt to study natural language behaviour. If readers are given access to the original data, in the form of transcripts of recorded speech, they can study these directly and propose alternative interpretations if necessary.

One reason, then, why researchers have fought shy of studying classroom interaction is the notorious complexity of communicative behaviour. But complexity will not dissolve if we ignore it. The drunk who loses his key along a dark stretch of the street has no hope of finding it under a lamp post just because the light is better there. The light may be bright in tests or experiments in the psychological laboratory, but it may not illuminate what we want to see. Complexity must therefore be admitted as an essential feature of social interaction and studied in its own right, with the help of appropriate concepts. In any case teacher–pupil dialogue is less complex than many other types of discourse, since it is often highly controlled in some fairly obvious ways.

5.4 Teachers as researchers

The type of work on classroom language which will now be discussed in the next two chapters is therefore very much work in progress. On the other hand, it comprises observations and analyses of the real, day-to-day classroom behaviour of teachers and pupils. One reason why little educational research is read by teachers is probably that hardly any of it is related in any obvious way to events in the classroom jungle. Practising teachers are clearly not in a position to do large-scale surveys or educational experiments involving laboratory facilities. But they *are* able to observe what happens inside classrooms. (Ch. 9 provides a list of specific suggestions.) Classroom research therefore comprises insights which any student or experienced teacher can verify, amend or refute every time he or she is in a classroom. Indeed it is theoretically important that practising teachers should do so. Research on children and classrooms is usually done by outsiders, but ultimately it is only the participants in a situation who have full access to all its relevant aspects. Ultimately, a sociolinguistic description of classroom language must come to grips with the values, attitudes and socially loaded meanings which are conveyed by the language, and only the participants have full access to these values. So, as Hymes puts it, 'The ethnography of a situation is not for a nonparticipant to say' (1972), since aspects of the communication situation in a classroom will often be quite opaque to an outsider (see Ch. 6.3). Conversely, however, as I have argued throughout, intuitive comments on language by insiders may well go astray, unless related to well thought out sociolinguistic concepts.

To say, then, that teachers themselves have an important part to play in studies of classroom language is not merely conventional courtesy. Quite simply, if the study of classroom language

97

has to wait on outside researchers, it will never happen in most classrooms. Hopefully, having read what follows, teachers and student teachers will be able to record and observe classroom lessons and notice new things. Linguists are rightly reticent about telling teachers how to behave in classrooms. But it *is* the task of linguists to provide educationalists with the means of observing and describing classroom language, and to indicate where they may look in language for educationally interesting findings. Chapters 6 and 7 can be read, therefore, as a collection of suggestions about how sociologists or teachers themselves can study classroom language, and Chapter 9 will provide a list of quite specific suggestions about how beginners to classroom research might start collecting and analysing data on classroom language.

6

Studies of classroom language

In one sense teachers *are* teachers: that is their job. But a person cannot simply walk into a classroom and *be* a teacher: he or she has to *do* quite specific communicative acts, such as lecturing, explaining, asking questions, encouraging pupils to speak and so on. In other words, social roles such as 'teacher' and 'pupil' do not exist in the abstract. They have to be acted out, performed and continuously constructed in the course of social interaction.

It is only since about 1970 that descriptions of classroom interaction have begun to appear. Such studies of classroom language are all in different ways fragmentary, but they contain interesting insights into the ways in which teachers and pupils communicate in real classrooms. And it is these insights which practising teachers can verify or amend from their own class-room experiences and observations. The studies to be discussed here are mainly small case-studies: of a single day's lessons or just of a single lesson, perhaps. So, only guarded claims are being made about teaching in general. On the other hand, behaviour at this level is often highly repetitive and subject to severe cultural constraints. And the state of the art at present requires detailed study of small amounts of data, rather than more superficial study of many hundreds of hours of classroom lessons.

All such studies, then, assume that close and *direct* study of classroom language will provide the most useful insights into teaching and learning processes. They maintain, at least implicitly, that general statements and theories of education will ultimately stand or fall according to whether they can explain how teachers and pupils communicate with each other in real classrooms. For, despite the large literature on 'learning theory', *how* and *what* children actually learn what they do in school remains almost a total mystery. In discussing such studies, it is well to bear in mind, however, that merely moving closer to *where* the action is, does not necessarily lead to *understanding* the action. For this, we need not mere surface descriptions of behaviour, but descriptions related to a coherent set of concepts: a theoretical framework in which to make sense of our observations.

6.1 Commentaries on classroom dialogue

A well known early study of classroom language is by Barnes (1969). It discusses extracts from tape-recordings of a day's lessons of a first-year class in a comprehensive school. The research is not systematic, but has many interesting points to make, based closely on quoted dialogue from actual lessons. The general theme of the study is the effect of teachers' language on pupils, particularly in situations where a teacher's language might be a barrier to learning, because the teachers use terminology or an abstract style of language with which the pupils are unfamiliar. The work is easily available, full of good examples of classroom talk, and a good introduction to anyone interested in the area.

One of Barnes's main arguments is concerned with a teacher's overall style of language. He argues that many teachers, in talking about their subject, use a specialist language of instruction which may be a barrier to pupils who are not used to it. This

100

specialist language, which may amount to a 'language of secondary education', has different aspects. First, different academic subjects have different technical terminologies associated with them. Teachers are usually aware of difficulties caused by this and will take care to present and define new terms, but sometimes such name-teaching seems to take on a value of its own. Thus one science teacher insisted on using the term 'mortar' (as in 'mortar and pestle'). Clearly, this term is not essential to understanding the subject, but is simply part of a whole scientific style of language in which the *teacher* feels at home. Such language makes linguistic demands on pupils which are quite extrinsic to the subject being taught. In other words, the *style* of language may prevent the content from getting through, and may prevent some pupils from contributing to the classroom dialogue.

A more subtle point Barnes makes is that many teachers may be unaware of a more pervasive language of secondary education, which is not part of the language of any particular academic subject and therefore likely never to be explained to pupils. One quote is from a history teacher, talking about city states:

> These states were complete in themselves because the terrain between cities was so difficult that it was hard for them to communicate. . . . Now because people lived like this in their own cities they tended to be intensely patriotic. . . .

The teacher uses the word *terrain* where *land* would do just as well. But he also talks in abstractions likely to be unfamiliar to first-form pupils: *complete in themselves, communicate, tended,* leaving the pupils to fill in from their own experience what might be meant in concrete terms. For example, 'tendency' is a complex, abstract, statistical notion, but unlikely to be taught by any teacher.

Because teachers are accustomed to such language, they may not recognize a valid idea from a pupil if it is not expressed in this abstract style (see Ch. 1.2). Thus, one science teacher had asked how a chlorophyll stain might be removed from material, and a pupil had suggested rubbing in shoe polish, then washing it all off. As the pupil did not use (or know?) the term 'solvent' or the name of a particular solvent, the teacher failed to see that he had in fact grasped the idea of a solvent and rejected the suggestion.

One general and very important point Barnes makes is as follows. A teacher may see the language of his subject as having an intellectual function of allowing concepts to be precisely expressed. But the teacher's language will also have a *sociocultural function* of supporting his or her role as teacher. And, from the pupils' point of view, each new term may have a predominantly sociocultural function: it is 'the sort of thing my teacher says'. Barnes is here pointing to a source of *sociolinguistic interference* between pupils and teachers who have different notions of stylistic conventions. That is, a teacher may use a certain style of language, not because it is necessary for expressing certain ideas, but because it is conventional to use it. But the pupils are unlikely to share these conventions. Conversely, the teacher may reject a pupil's formulation, not because the pupil's language is intrinsically unable to express an idea, but because it does not accord with stylistic conventions.

A second topic of great general importance is Barnes's preliminary classification of the kinds of questions teachers ask. He distinguishes four broad categories of questions: (1) *factual* (what?) questions which demand a bit of information or a name for something; (2) *reasoning* (how? or why?) questions which might demand observation, recalling something from memory, or more open-ended reasoning; (3) *open* questions, not demanding reasoning; and (4) *social* questions, functioning either to control the class or appealing to them to share in some experience. This part of the analysis is very loose, and Barnes admits that the categories are not precise enough for use by others. However, it usefully points to the difficulty of matching the form of a teacher's question to the underlying intention or function. Thus a teacher may ask a question which appears superficially to be asking a pupil for his personal view, when the teacher really has a particular answer in mind. Barnes calls such utterances 'pseudo questions'.

Barnes admits that his study is 'impressionistic' (p. 47), that he has no objective way of describing the language of secondary education (p. 53), and that his classification of different types of question is vague. Since the study is intended to be of practical use to teachers rather than a contribution to theory, this is not necessarily an outright condemnation. As a whole, one could call the method insightful observation. Note, however, the positive points that the study is based on *recording and observation of normal school lessons*, and that Barnes presents extracts from the records. Readers are therefore able, to some extent at least, to study the data directly and to propose alternative interpretations if they disagree with Barnes's intuitions.

In other work, Barnes (1971) has pointed to some implications of such descriptive studies of classroom language. He begins from the statement that 'language is a means of learning'. That is, we often learn, not only by passively listening to a teacher, but by actively discussing, talking a question through, defending our views in debate and so on. By studying teacher–pupil interaction, one can therefore study how classroom language opens and closes different learning possibilities to pupils. Do they have to sit passively listening, providing answers on demand? Or is there active, two-way dialogue between teacher and pupil? These topics deserve a whole chapter, and will be taken up again below, in Chapter 7.

A study by Mishler (1972) is similar to Barnes's in that it comprises perceptive commentary on fragments of classroom dialogue. But Mishler is more concerned with specifying which particular features of language are indicators of different teaching strategies. He shows that the particulars of actual language used by teachers and pupils can be analysed in ways which yield information about important aspects of the educational process; arguing that what teachers say and how they say it creates a particular kind of world for pupils. The study is based on recordings of three first-grade American teachers.

He argues first – an important theme of the present book – that studies of language in use must present data in a form which is open to reanalysis by readers. A minimal requirement for this

103

is a verbatim transcript of tape-recorded talk. Mishler's main aim is then to specify how different teachers' cognitive strategies are displayed (betrayed?) in the fine details of classroom dialogue: that is, to specify features of teachers' language which indicate to pupils how information and concepts should be organized, and therefore direct their attention to different forms of order in the world. For example, a teacher's use of open-ended questions (e.g. 'What could that mean?') may imply the underlying pedagogic message that different answers are acceptable: not an assumption made in all classrooms (see Ch. 7.3). Conversely, he shows how a teacher may deny the legitimacy of what a child says. A child asks about a film the class is going to see:

C: What's it about?
T: I don't think I'm going to tell you.

In fact, the teacher has not seen the film, but she does not admit this. She uses a type of exchange which denies the child access to knowledge and maintains the teacher as the only person who knows, and who controls what the pupil may know. (An English lecturer at a Midlands university once told me with some glee that, in a seminar on Jane Austen, he had asked 'Who does Lydia Bennett marry?', knowing that this would be understood by students as a test question – whereas he really asked the question to fill in his own knowledge as he had not finished the book and did not know the answer!)

Mishler's approach is one which could be of direct interest to teachers. By close study of transcribed lessons he shows how quite general teaching strategies are conveyed by the fine grain of a teacher's use of language. Such a study can therefore begin to throw a little light on how children learn what they do in school. Only by close observation of how teachers and pupils actually talk to each other can one discover how concepts are put across, how some lines of inquiry are opened up and others closed off, how pupils' responses are evaluated, and how their attention is directed to the areas of knowledge which the school regards as valuable.

A study by Gumperz and Herasimchuk (1972) is similar in style to Mishler's. It is based on a commentary on just two tape-recorded lessons, chosen so as to be maximally different: a teacher teaching a group of pupils, and an older child (aged 6) teaching a younger child (aged 5). By close study of the recordings and transcripts, the authors show that the adult and child use different means of communication. For example, the adult teacher relies heavily on interrogatives to elicit answers from pupils, and makes use of variation in choice of words with a corresponding lack of variation in intonation. The child teacher makes more use of intonational variety and repetition, especially to distinguish questions, challenges and confirmations, and to maintain an extraordinary degree of musical and rhythmical relatedness with the pupil. That is, they show the child and adult teachers using different means of communication.

They claim further that the adult and child differ in their definition of the teaching task and of the social relationships involved. But this does not seem to follow from the evidence they present. They seem rather to have found the two 'teachers' *doing* similar things (questioning, challenging, confirming) by *means* of different linguistic devices.

It would be most useful to teachers if they could be made more aware of the linguistic means by which children may communicate messages, especially where these differ from adult usage. Gumperz and Herasimchuk place useful emphasis on the precise linguistic signals which convey social messages in the classroom, and show that these signs may not only be the words or sentences used, but the way utterances are sequenced, and the paralinguistic signs such as intonation and rhythm.

In work of my own (Stubbs, 1976) I have described one way in which teachers in relatively formal chalk-and-talk lessons keep control over the classroom discourse. One thing which characterizes much classroom talk is the extent to which the teacher has *conversational control* over the topic, over the relevance or correctness of what pupils say, and over when and how much pupils may speak. In traditional chalk-and-talk lessons, pupils have correspondingly few conversational rights. This has often been pointed out in general (e.g. by Barnes, 1969), but the actual verbal strategies which teachers use to control classroom talk have yet to be systematically described.

Teachers' talk in such lessons is characterized by the way the teacher constantly explains things, corrects pupils, evaluates and edits their language, summarizes the discussion and controls the direction of the lesson. That is, a teacher is constantly monitoring the communication system in the classroom, by checking whether pupils are all on the same wavelength and whether at least some of the pupils follow what the teacher is saying. Such monitoring may actually comprise what we understand by 'teaching'. It is useful to refer to such language as *metacommunication*. It is communication about communication: messages which refer back to the communication system itself, checking whether it is functioning properly. Suppose, for example, a teacher says, *Now don't start now, just listen*. He is not here saying anything substantive, but merely attracting the pupils' attention, opening the communication channels and preparing them for messages to come. Or he might say, *You see, we're really getting on to the topic now*, again not adding anything to the content of the discussion, but commenting on the state of the discussion itself. Or again, he might control the amount of pupils' speech by saying, *Some of you are not joining in the studious silence we are trying to develop*. Teachers exert control over different aspects of the communication system in the classroom. They control the channels of communication by opening and closing them: *OK now listen all of you*. They control the amount of talk by asking pupils to speak or keep quiet: *Colin, what were you going to say?* They control the content of the talk and define the relevance of what is said: *Now, we don't want any silly remarks*. They control the language forms used: *That's not English*. And they try to control understanding: *Who knows what this means?*

All the italicized examples are taken from recorded classroom lessons. The metacommunicative remarks can be generally formally recognized by the use of metalinguistic terms which refer to the ongoing discourse itself, e.g. *listen, topic, say, remarks*, etc.

Such talk is characteristic of teachers' language: utterances which, as it were, stand outside the discourse and comment on it comprise a large percentage of what teachers say to their pupils, and comprise a major way of controlling classroom dialogue. Use of such language is also highly asymmetrical: one would not expect a pupil to say to a teacher: *That's an interesting point*. Such speech acts, in which the teacher monitors and controls the classroom dialogue are, at one level, the very stuff of teaching. They are basic to the activity of teaching, since they are the acts whereby a teacher *controls the flow of information* in the classroom and defines the relevance of what is said (see Atkinson, 1975; and Ch. 7.5).

6.2 The structure of classroom dialogue

Detailed commentary on small fragments of teacher–pupil dialogue is clearly a necessary step in work on classroom language. But one also wants to go beyond commentary on the details of small excerpts torn from their conversational context, and to make more comprehensive statements about how classroom talk works as a *system* of communication. There is a clear need, then, to pay close attention to the fine details of what teachers and pupils actually say. On the other hand, it is not enough to make insightful comments on short extracts, selecting, according to intuition, extracts which seem interesting and ignoring the rest. It is necessary to work towards generalizations about classroom discourse. The next two studies discussed attempt to do this.

Rather than focusing on the fine details of teacher–pupil dialogue, Bellack *et al.* (1966) argue that much teacher–pupil talk has a characteristic *underlying structure* and pattern which teachers and pupils follow with remarkably little deviation. Their analysis is based on a coding of transcribed audiorecordings of about sixty classes. They start from Wittgenstein's notion of a language game, in which speakers follow rules and conventions. They propose four pedagogical *moves* as basic units of classroom dialogue: *structuring* moves indicate the direction the speaker thinks the discussion should take; *soliciting* moves serve to elicit a response from another speaker; *responding* moves bear a reciprocal relationship to soliciting moves (e.g. a pupil's answer to a teacher's question); and *reacting* moves modify or clarify a preceding utterance. These moves are a preliminary definition of how teacher–pupil discourse works: they define possible sequences of teacher–pupil talk.

The moves are analysed as building up into repetitive teaching *cycles*; cycles build up, in turn, into *sub-games*, and sub-games into *games*. Overall rules which they propose for the classroom dialogue are: that the teacher is the most active player; that, in general, the game is played within the teacher's structure; that the teacher's primary role is solicitor while the pupil's is respondent. They discovered, for example, that fifteen teachers made 50 per cent more moves than 345 pupils, that the core of the game was the solicit–response pattern (this was slightly more than three-fifths of all moves made), and that the pupils were mainly confined to responding.

This study is therefore a preliminary attempt not simply to describe what teachers and pupils say and how they say it, in terms of individual utterances: it is an attempt to formulate a hierarchical structure for classroom discourse, an abstract and general model to which the actual classroom talk conforms in varying degrees. The work by Bellack *et al.* is thus a preliminary attempt to study the overall *structure* of teacher–pupil dialogue. This approach is taken much further by Sinclair and Coulthard (1975).

Sinclair and Coulthard are linguists and primarily interested in studying types of linguistic patterning in long texts collected by tape-recording spontaneous conversation between several speakers. Their work is one of the few attempts to provide an analysis of the underlying structure of classroom dialogue and there is much in it of interest to educationalists.

The easiest way to explain some of their main ideas is to begin with a piece of their data.

```
T: What makes a road slippery?                        (1)
P: You might have rain or snow on it.                 (2)
T: Yes, snow, ice.
   Anything else make a road slippery?                (3)
P: Erm, oil.                                          (4)
T: Oil makes it slippery when it's mixed with
   water doesn't it?                                  (5)
```

There are five utterances in this teacher–pupil interchange, but intuitively we feel that there is an obvious boundary in the middle of (3), corresponding to the line division after *ice*. Further we might feel that there are just two conversational units: T *asks question* – P *responds* – T *evaluates*, and a repeat of this unit. Sinclair and Coulthard propose that this *exchange structure* is a typical one in many classrooms. They propose that it is a basic type of *teaching exchange*, and label its constituent parts: (teacher's) *initiation*, (pupil's) *response* and (teacher's) *feedback*, or IRF for short. The constituent parts they call *moves*: that is, exchanges consist of moves. Another type of teaching exchange is illustrated by data such as:

```
T: Finished Joan?                   I
P: (Nods)                           R
T: Good girl.                       F
   And Miri?                        I
P: Yes.                             R
T: Good.                            F
   Finished?                        I
P: Yes.                             R
```

Here a teacher *initiation* is followed by a pupil *response*, and sometimes by a teacher *feedback*. So the exchange structure is IR(F), where brackets indicate an optional item. A different exchange structure occurs when a pupil asks a question. Here the structure is IR, with no F, since pupils do not generally overtly evaluate teachers' answers! In many classrooms (but not all) pupils' initiations are largely restricted to procedural matters such as, 'Can I leave the room?' or 'Do we have to use coloured pencils?' Sinclair and Coulthard propose several other types of teaching exchange, but these examples will suffice to illustrate the type of analysis.

So, exchanges consist of moves (I, R and F). But *moves* are often further analysable into *acts*. Thus it seems inadequate to call this teacher's utterance an initiation and leave it at that:

> T: A group of people used symbols in their writing,
>   they used pictures instead of words.   (1)
>   Do you know who those people were?   (2)
>   I'm sure you do.   (3)
>   Joan.   (4)

The proposed structure here is: (1) *starter*, (2) *elicitation*, (3) *prompt*, (4) *nomination*; where these labels name *acts* which comprise the teacher's opening *move* in an *exchange*.

As well as teaching exchanges, one also comes across utterances such as,

> T: Well, today I thought we'd do three quizzes.

Here the teacher is providing an opening *boundary* to the talk: not yet teaching anything, but announcing that the lesson is under way and indicating the direction it will go. So, Sinclair and Coulthard propose a *boundary exchange* which has the move structure: *frame–focus*. *Frames* function to indicate boundaries in lessons and are realized by a small number of words: *well, right, good, OK, now*. A *focus* functions to indicate where the lesson is going.

Boundary exchanges therefore indicate that lessons are further structured into larger units, which Sinclair and Coulthard call *transactions*. They are therefore proposing a hierarchic and structural analysis of teacher–pupil talk. The *lesson* consists of *transactions*, marked off by boundary exchanges. Transactions consist of *exchanges*, an initial boundary exchange, then teaching exchanges of different types. Exchanges consist of *moves* which consist of *acts*.

These units of discourse are functional units which specify what a speaker is using language for: e.g. to mark a boundary in the discourse or to evaluate a pupil's answer. The relationship between such language functions and the language forms which realize them is very complex. Sinclair and Coulthard provide a good example of the type of complexity involved. A class have been listening to a tape-recording of a speaker with a 'posh' accent. One of the pupils laughs, and the teacher says: 'What are you laughing at?' The pupil takes this as a criticism and as a command to stop laughing, whereas the teacher intends it as a genuine question, an opening move to explore the children's attitudes. That is, the pupil has misunderstood a particular language form, a *what* interrogative, as a command instead of a question.

Fuller accounts of Sinclair and Coulthard's work are provided by Burton (1980), Stubbs, Robinson and Twite (1979), Stubbs (1983), Willes (in press) and by articles in French and MacLure (1981).

6.3 The classroom as a sociolinguistic setting

Classroom dialogue requires study as a linguistic system. This is likely to be the area in which linguists will make the largest contribution. But it must also be remembered that classroom talk is not merely a linguistic system, but a sociolinguistic system.

Walker and Adelman (1975a and b, 1976) regard classrooms as intense and complex social settings. They have been particularly interested in different types of *social organization* in classrooms and in different kinds of social control and personal relationships which the language between teachers and pupils can sustain. They point out that much research (e.g. the studies discussed earlier in this chapter) has concentrated on 'formal' classrooms in which the teacher stands at the front of the class and has the attention of the whole class. But there is little work on 'informal' or 'open' classrooms where children are working in small groups, the teacher passing from group to group or talking to individual children. They see such situations as crucially different.

Walker and Adelman's research in such classrooms has opened up important issues for the theory and methodology of observing life in classrooms. In particular, they emphasize the dangers of too narrow a notion of classroom language. If one transcribes teacher–pupil dialogue from a formal chalk-and-talk lesson, the transcript characteristically looks like a conventional playscript: speakers down the left and relatively well-formed language on the right. Such transcripts are generally easy to understand, even for the reader who has no information about the context of the recording. (See, for example, most of the dialogue extracts in the present book.) However, sound-recordings from informal contexts are typically not completely comprehensible without a *visual* record of the classroom. In transcript, the talk appears fragmented, incomplete, full of hesitations, interruptions and ambiguities. It is difficult to know who is talking to whom, and what is being talked about. But this is a mere surface description: these characteristics do not appear as defects to the participants, who can fill in their understanding from gestures, facial expressions, postures and the surrounding situation.

One way of putting this is to say that in informal classrooms the talk is strongly context bound. That is, its understanding depends on a knowledge of the context in which it was recorded, and, ultimately, on the culture of the class. An example will make this clear. A teacher has been listening to a pupil read a rather skimpy piece of work:

T: Is that all you've done?
P: Strawberries! Strawberries!

(Walker and Adelman, 1976). This exchange only makes sense if we know that the teacher has previously said to the pupils that their work was 'like strawberries – OK as far as it goes, but it doesn't last long enough'. It is simply not possible to retrieve such meanings from the transcript alone.

Walker and Adelman are making a crucial point: the meanings of classroom language are often not as simple as they seem. The talk often cannot be taken at its face value or commonsense meaning. They are thus criticizing the naïve and impoverished concept of classroom language, which is implicit in some studies, by emphasizing in particular the inherent complexity of meanings which may develop between speakers over long periods of time. Such meanings are part of the shared culture of the class and may be hidden from a casual observer. Most important, they point out that talk may have quite *different functions* in formal and informal classrooms. In formal classrooms, the talk may be primarily concerned with transmitting information. But in informal classrooms, the talk also has to sustain complex social relationships during intimate, small group discussions or one-to-one teacher–pupil talk.

Methodologically and theoretically, Walker and Adelman are concerned to develop new ways of thinking about teachers and pupils in classrooms. Their most important innovation here is a system of stop-frame cinematography developed for filming in schools. Using this system, photographs can be taken at intervals of, say, every 2 or 3 seconds, and synchronized with a sound recording. The timing of the photographs is not arbitrary, however. In primary classrooms it is typically necessary to take photographs more frequently, approximately every second, in order to preserve enough visual information to allow a viewer to make sense of the sound recording. That is, the recording technique, in itself, tells us something about the activities in different classrooms.

From the perspective of the other studies discussed in this chapter, Walker and Adelman leave their linguistic data underanalysed. But they warn workers in the area of several pitfalls. They show how talk can sustain radically different concepts of social relationships. They question the view that all classrooms have a peculiar common structure and ask whether this view simply means that research has only looked at a narrow range of classrooms. And they emphasize the complexity of meanings underlying classroom dialogue, many of which may be hidden without an understanding of the classrooms in which the dialogue is recorded.

6.4 Studying social processes in classrooms

Other studies of classroom language could be reviewed, but the reader will by now have a sufficient idea of the kind of work that has been done.

Studies of classroom language are, as yet, a mixed collection of exploratory work on a relatively narrow range of classrooms, and some general limitations of such work will be discussed in Chapter 8. Nevertheless, several important findings keep turning up in different studies. Much work, for example, has pointed to the highly assymmetrical control which teachers often maintain over classroom dialogue, dominating the talk both by the amount of their own talk, and also by the use of certain discourse sequences (e.g. IRF). Many studies also comment on teachers' characteristic use of 'questions' which are not genuine requests for information. These are variously called test questions (by Labov), pseudo questions and closed questions (by Barnes), and convergent and guess-what-I'm-thinking questions (by Postman and Weingartner). It is worthwhile pondering the effect on classroom dialogue when some teachers rarely ask questions because they want to know something! These two findings point to the highly artificial nature of much teacher–pupil dialogue, compared to, say, casual conversation between social equals.

One thing which is clear from studying teacher–pupil interaction is just how constrained it often is by cultural rules. The question–answer pattern, for example, has been found to have been stable over the past fifty years (Hoetker and Ahlbrandt, 1969) and across different countries (Bellack, 1973), although it has regularly been criticized by educational theorists. Work on classroom language therefore begins to make explicit some of the sociolinguistic demands made on pupils, and to give further substance to the general finding cited earlier (Ch. 4.3) that the social situation is the strongest determinant of verbal behaviour.

The most fundamental aspect of work on classroom language is therefore as follows. Out of the vast body of educational research, only a small fragment inquires into the *social processes* which occur in schools and classrooms. Research has often reflected educators' definitions of education. It has therefore taken as its problem to discover how to teach pupils better or faster, taking for granted underlying assumptions about the aims of education. But the question of *what* is learned has often been bypassed by research which has thus been designed to measure pupils before and after some predefined teaching process. Direct analysis of the teaching process itself can, however, enable the nature of the process to be studied. One can study, for example, how social control and discipline are maintained in classrooms: not taking for granted that they should be maintained, but studying just how the trick is done (Torode, 1976). Or one can study how different forms of teacher–pupil dialogue inevitably imply sociocultural relations between teacher and pupil as well as conveying intellectual messages. In a word, one can begin to study how children are transformed into pupils (Willes, in press).

Note a point which is often misunderstood. We are here concerned with analysing what goes on in classrooms, and with discovering some of the sociolinguistic pressures at work there. We are not concerned with prejudging what goes on as either good or bad. The argument for or against the value of question–answer techniques should be considered *separately*.

The sociolinguistic situation in classrooms and tests

We can, however, point to the effect of certain dialogue situations on the verbal behaviour which is likely to be observed. Work on classroom language is thus immediately relevant to the earlier discussion (see Ch. 4.3) of how children's verbal competence is to be judged. We now have more precise sociolinguistic reasons why such teacher–pupil (and, more generally, adult–pupil) dialogue is typically a quite misleading context in which to measure a child's linguistic capacity. The rules of classroom dialogue are often quite distinct from conversation between social equals, and the pupil often learns, for example, to give short answers to discrete questions and not to initiate discussion: in other words, he often learns a predominantly passive role. In many classrooms (but not all) this is what it *means* to acquire the role of 'pupil'. In such situations, pupils will therefore not easily be encouraged to drop well-learned conversational roles and to display the kinds of linguistic competence which they may well typically display in quite different sociolinguistic situations with their social peers. Evidence from several independent studies (e.g. Labov, 1969; Wight, 1975; Barnes and Todd, 1977) has indicated that teacher absence can often lead to productive and complex discussion among children.

The artificial nature of much teacher–pupil dialogue (in which pupils tell the teacher what he or she already knows) is analogous to the lack of any real communicative purpose in many test situations in which a child may have to tell a story about a series of pictures (see Ch. 3.2). Different types of work have, however, shown that children's language often becomes more complex and effective when they have to deal with real communicative tasks: either as part of communication games (Wight, 1975; see Ch. 4.5) or in talking about situations which are important to them (Labov, 1969).

It is also clear that a child will be unable to display his total verbal competence if he is restricted to a passive response role, sandwiched between the teacher's initiation and feedback. The child must also have the opportunity to initiate discussion. It is therefore clear that if the status relations between adult and child are highly asymmetrical, the child's language will characteristically be much less complex than in conversation with social equals.

We must therefore be very aware of the sociolinguistic pressures which operate in traditional teacher–pupil or tester–pupil situations, and thus of the precise limitations on assessing children's linguistic competence in such settings: limitations which result from widely shared norms of speech behaviour in our culture. To summarize: if we want to begin to tap something approaching a representative range of a child's verbal capacity we must construct test situations which comprise *at least* the

116

following factors. The language tasks must have *real communicative purpose*. (Ideally we would have to observe the child in real, that is naturally occurring, social situations outside the classroom.) The rules which govern adult–child talk will often place the child in a responding role. He will therefore only be able to display certain verbal skills in a situation *with his social equals*, in which he can *initiate* discussions as well as respond. If we do not take such factors into account, verbal 'tests' will simply generate verbal incompetence in children by repressing precisely those aspects of linguistic proficiency they claim to measure.

7

Teaching and talking: the hidden curriculum of classroom talk

There is no reason why educationalists should be interested in classroom language for its own sake. But analyses of classroom discourse become interesting when they can be shown to be sensitive to educationally relevant issues. It is important, however, not to expect such educational relevance to lie too near the surface. It would be naïve, for example, to expect comparative studies of different types of teacher–pupil dialogue to reveal that one single type of classroom interaction produces better, faster or more efficient learning than others. Research has never revealed a clear correlation between styles of classroom dialogue and 'teaching effectiveness'. Nor is this surprising, since all teachers know they have to change their style of teaching according to such imponderable factors as the topic of the lesson and the mood of the class.

It is possible, however, to study classroom discourse in terms of the *meanings* it conveys to pupils, and thus to investigate much more fundamental questions: what knowledge *is* transmitted from teachers to pupils? and *what counts as educational knowledge?*

7.1 The hidden curriculum

Recent work in the sociology of knowledge (e.g. Young, 1971) has emphasized the need to study how knowledge is selected, organized and transmitted in schools, since it is clear that *what counts as knowledge* is not decidable a priori. School examinations and timetables define for the pupil what is legitimate, examinable, educational knowledge: this might include, for example, literature but not cinema, Greek myths but not British folk culture. But little is known about *how* what counts as knowledge is defined in schools and made available to pupils.

One way of studying just how knowledge is organized in the classroom is to study classroom discourse in some of the ways I have illustrated in the previous chapter. By studying the sequencing and structure of teacher–pupil dialogue, we can study in empirical detail how teachers divide knowledge into discrete 'topics'; how they relate one topic to another; how they present knowledge as discrete 'facts' or as more open-ended suggestions and hypotheses; how they evaluate pupils' contributions as correct or appropriate; how they control what it is relevant to talk about in classrooms, and so on. In fact, *only* by studying teacher–pupil dialogue directly can we fully study the mechanics of how knowledge comes to be defined and transmitted to pupils. There are, of course, other aspects of how knowledge comes to be defined: one might study from this point of view the implementation of new curricula (Hamilton, 1976).

The term 'hidden curriculum' is used by some authors (Jackson, 1968; Snyder, 1971) to mean the tacit values and attitudes concerning appropriate pupil behaviour which all pupils must learn if they are to be successful at school: values concerning what is appropriate educational knowledge, what are appropriate pupil responses to teachers' questions, and so on. Many such messages are transmitted to pupils, but they are rarely transmitted explicitly in the content of what teachers say. Neither, however, are they transmitted mystically or by osmosis. When people are asked how it is that children acquire values and attitudes, they often say that such values are 'absorbed'

119

from parents and friends: I usually refer to this as the blotting-paper theory of culture. It is not, however, a real theory, since it leaves totally unexplained *how* values are absorbed, or from where. It should be clear from the last chapter that many tacit messages are transmitted by the *form* and *structure* of teacher–pupil dialogue.

Few writers on the classroom have emphasized how regularly the teacher defines and redefines the classroom situation. Jackson (1968) points out that children spend over a thousand hours per year in school: which amounts to some ten thousand hours by the time they leave, at least. And for most of this time the teacher may be talking! In addition, school classrooms are often rather standardized and routine places: a constant, ritualized, stylized environment. It would be strange indeed if the very organization of all this teacher talk did not hammer home time after time taken-for-granted assumptions and expectations concerning appropriate teacher and pupil behaviour. The medium has ten thousand hours to convey its message.

For example, Barnes (1969) found that three (English, history and religious education) teachers used many more questions demanding facts than reasoning. That is, there were many questions of the type, 'What books did Homer write?', and few questions requiring pupils to think things out for themselves. Barnes points out that a covert message being transmitted to pupils is that information is more important than original thought. The teachers never say this explicitly: the message is not conveyed in the *content* of what they say. The message is implicit in the *form* of the whole teacher–pupil dialogue. In the relative proportion of different types of questions asked is a covert message about the nature of the subject being taught. Of course, the teacher may be quite unaware of this message, but this does not prevent pupils from receiving it.

We can phrase this point slightly more generally as follows. By studying the details of teacher–pupil dialogue it is possible to get some insight into the participants' ideas about how educational knowledge should be transmitted, and therefore their conceptions of what 'teaching' consists of. A teacher's use of language in the classroom will serve to maintain a definition of the situation, not only by maintaining social control and underpinning social relations, but also by maintaining a specific concept of *what constitutes valid knowledge* and how this knowledge should be put across to pupils. In fact, there is no way in which maintaining social control and transmitting knowledge can be strictly separated (Young, 1971). In the classroom, we have a quite specific case where 'knowledge is power'. (Consider, in this connection, how revealing is the ambiguity in the expression 'academic discipline'!)

In other words, we can regard teaching, first, as a speech event with specific rules and expectations concerning appropriate teacher and pupil behaviour. Second, we can study these rules for what they reveal about underlying assumptions about how knowledge should be selected, organized and transmitted to pupils. This is, therefore, one way of providing a powerful definition of what 'teaching' means to teachers and pupils. The definition is powerful because it is grounded in detailed observations of the actual classroom speech of teachers and pupils. It is not a notion which has been thought up in the abstract, independent of actual teaching. Nor is it a notion derived, say, from interviewing teachers and/or pupils: that is, from second-hand accounts. Rather, it is possible to observe the details of actual teaching and to recover from such data certain assumptions about education.

7.2 The framing of educational knowledge

In Chapter 3 I criticized Bernstein for failing to relate his theory to observations of language in use, particularly in the classroom. Would it be possible to relate some of Bernstein's concepts to the kind of analysis of classroom language that I have proposed? It would seem important to try, for the latest collection of his papers, *Class, Codes and Control*, volume 3 (*CCC 3*), sets out to provide a framework for a 'theory of educational transmission'. This theory is seen as part of a more general 'theory of cultural transmission': a theory of how cultural norms and values are

121

passed on from one generation to the next, from parents and teachers to children. One of Bernstein's criticisms of American sociolinguistic work on education is that it has failed to provide any systematic theory of the transmission of educational knowledge (*CCC 3*, p. 29, and see Ch. 4.4 above).

In a major paper on this topic, Bernstein (1971b) discusses how educational knowledge is selected, classified, distributed, transmitted and evaluated. The way a school timetable is divided into different academic subjects, and how these subjects are presented and paced, is often taken for granted. But, of course, there are many different ways of selecting what should be taught, when and how. Innovations, such as Nuffield science, integrated or interdisciplinary studies, have often brought into question how educational knowledge itself is defined. Bernstein proposes three 'message systems' through which educational knowledge is transmitted: *curriculum* defines what counts as valid knowledge; *pedagogy* defines what counts as valid transmission of knowledge; and *evaluation* defines what counts as valid realizations of this knowledge on the pupil's part. In the last chapter, I discussed, from my own point of view, pedagogy.

There are several concepts in Bernstein's paper which are beyond the scope of discussion here, although they are very important in their own right. The concept of Bernstein's most relevant to my discussion here is *frame*. This refers to the actual relationship between teachers and pupils, to the 'strength of the boundary between what may and may not be transmitted', and therefore to the range of choice teachers and pupils have over what is to be taught. Bernstein's discussion is entirely abstract, but an aspect of this control over knowledge could be studied in transcripts of teacher–pupil dialogue. According to Bernstein, 'strong frames reduce the power of the pupil over what, when and how he receives his knowledge'. Bernstein gives no examples at all to relate his concepts to observed classroom interaction, although he proposes that the concepts can be used at the level of classroom encounters (*CCC 3*, p. 8). But I have already illustrated in detail how a study of classroom dialogue can investigate the specific mechanisms by which knowledge is transmitted and paced. A teacher, for example, whose predominant teaching strategy involve strings of IRF exchanges would be a very strong framer (see Ch. 6.2).

Bernstein has referred to his work as a 'theory of the structure of cultural transmission'. One way in which he explains the success of many MC children at school is to refer to the 'continuity of culture' between home and school. But precisely *what* is transmitted and *how*, and just what this 'continuity' comprises, is never made entirely clear. There are many levels at which such 'continuity' might exist and could be investigated. Continuity of culture (just restricting ourselves to cognitive/verbal culture) might refer to many things: to the presence of books in the home; to the use of the same standard dialect at home and in school; to the use of the same elaborated code; or to playing the same discourse games. Consider this extract of mother–child dialogue. The child is 4 years old, and they are cooking together:

M: Right, now – what do you think the next instruction is because that's what I've got to do?
C: Put it in the baking tin.
M: Yes.
Well, first of all we've got to grease it though – why, do you think? Why do you grease it Tommy?
C: So the pastry doesn't stick.
M: Right.

The discourse structure here is identical to some of the teacher–pupil dialogue discussed above. The mother is asking 'test questions' to check if the child knows certain things, and the conversation is quite incidental to the cooking. (Imagine the absurdity of this conversation between husband and wife, instead of between child and mother!) It is a purely verbal game, a knowledge game, which fits the IRF pattern. Clearly, this child will have no difficulty in recognizing the same game if it is played at school. This may then identify one specific level of communicative behaviour at which culture is transmitted.

Adults talking to children often ask test questions to which they know the answer. Thus the following interchange overheard in a café, between an adult and a girl aged about 4 years:

A: What's my name?
C: (Smiles)
A: Is it Brian?
C: No.
A: What is it?
C: David.
A: Yes!

The child may well have been smiling politely at the lunacy of the question. Again imagine the absurdity of this interchange between two adults. Our society has characteristic ways of talking to its children.

I do not wish here to make premature generalizations. On the contrary, I am saying that such topics have hardly been investigated. There is an almost total lack of field studies of how educational knowledge is transmitted (although Barnes, 1969; Keddie, 1971; Furlong, 1976; Gannaway, 1976; Delamont, 1983 are a start). But it is possible to study, for example, some specific ways in which the culture of home and school may be continuous or not, and to relate such high-level concepts as 'strength of frame' to actual observed and recorded interaction. Wells *et al.* (1981) is the first volume of an important series which studies children's language at home and at school on the basis of a large amount of tape-recorded data collected over some ten years.

7.3 Discourse structure and assumptions about teaching

What we are concerned with, then, is messages which may be transmitted by the structure and sequencing of teacher–pupil discourse, and the ways in which teaching and learning roles are defined.

As a specific example, consider some possible implications of the discourse structure IRF: *teacher initiates – pupil responds –*

teacher gives feedback (Sinclair and Coulthard, 1975; and Ch. 6.2). In dialogues of this IRF structure, the pupil's role is passive: he must respond. It is the teacher who initiates, and then evaluates the response before asking another closed question. This conversational structure gives the teacher almost complete control over initiating the topic, and over evaluating, accepting or rejecting the pupil's contribution, and thus over closing the exchange. Anything the pupil says is sandwiched between whatever the teacher says. Note just how basic are the assumptions underlying such a discourse structure: the assumption that it is the teacher who has control over who talks when; and that education consists of listening to an adult talking, and answering his or her questions. *If* classroom dialogue was constructed primarily from such exchanges, a general tacit message which might be transmitted by the three-part IRF structure is something like:

> Classroom knowledge consists of strings of short answers which can be individually evaluated. Classroom knowledge is therefore essentially closed, not open-ended. All questions have correct answers. Teacher–pupil talk is effectively a monologue with the pupil supplying short answers on demand to contribute to the teacher's train of thought.

These are the messages which pupils might receive from the *form* or *structure* of the dialogue, quite independently of the *content* of the dialogue. Note that the only other common conversational structure of the form question–answer–evaluation is a riddle! Some teacher–pupil dialogue is quite literally composed of little riddles where the pupils have to guess what particular word or expression the teacher is thinking of. Thus, an English teacher discussing a poem – his pupils have failed to use a particular word which he wants them to:

T: Well, I'm going to help you – a word beginning with A.
P: Attitudes.
T: Yes – now answer again using the word 'attitudes'.

Or, another example, the teacher has been discussing how one speaks to different people: in this case the pupils have failed to guess another particular word the teacher 'had in mind', as we often put it.

> T: 'Respect' – this is the word I wanted to come out earlier but it didn't – you have to speak 'respectfully' to a headmaster.

Or consider, more generally, the message pupils may get from teachers who never ask questions because they want to know something, but because they want pupils to display their knowledge. The message here might be: teachers know everything or, at least, everything that pupils know, and the pupil therefore has nothing new to tell the teacher. Of course, the teacher may not believe this, but this may be the message that the pupil receives, transmitted by the structure of the classroom dialogue. All teachers know that what they teach is not always what pupils learn!

Atkinson (1975) discusses the mutual pretence involved when teachers ask pupils questions to which they already know the answers. He suggests viewing such conversational situations as information games: they are simulations or 'mock-ups' in which the teacher is asking about his own knowledge, and organizing the classroom dialogue so that little bits of knowledge are allowed to emerge when the teacher considers it appropriate. He concludes that: 'The maintenance of reality based on the principle of discounting, suppressing or covering previously acquired knowledge may turn out to be a fundamental feature of instructional situations.'

Suppose, on the other hand, that teacher–pupil dialogue characteristically takes this form:

> (A discussion about corporal punishment has been underway for about 10 minutes.)
> T: You don't think corporal punishment is, er – in a school – you think corporal punishment is all right at home – but er, not in a school.

P1: No, I don't say that. I said until a certain level the cane I am against.

T: 'Until a certain level' – I don't understand you.

P1: Ah yes, I explained 10 minutes ago.

T: Well, I still don't – 'until a certain level', I don't – I don't quite understand what you mean.

P1: The cane I am against, slaps I am for.

T: Oh yeah – I see.

P2: I can't agree – if, er, a smack can do nothing.

T: A slap?

P2: A slap can do nothing if, er – I don't know – a text to learn by heart can do nothing.

T: You think that a text is just the same thing – thing to give, er – something like, em – lines – to write out or to learn – it's just the same thing?

P2: It's not the same thing – I don't say that – it has no more effect.

T: It has no more effect.

(The discussion continued with P2 telling a story about a friend of a friend who had committed suicide after being corporally punished in school. The teacher brought the discussion to a close as follows.)

T: Would you like to, er, say – sum up what you think about corporal punishment in general?

P1: In general?

T: Like to sum up, yeah – what you think now after this discussion – in a few words to say – what you think.

P1: I am still of the same opinion. I am against.

T: You're against corporal punishment.

P1: Yes.

T: And, er.

P1: There are too many bad consequences in the future for –

P2: But I keep the same opinion as the, er

T: You have the same opinion.

P2: Yes, because what you said – what you said – what you told us, it's nothing. I have destroyed – for me. I think that

127

     – it seems to me that – it seems for me that with the last
     example that I gave you, all your opinions are com – all
     your, em –
T: Arguments.
P2: Arguments are completely destroyed.
T: For you.
P2: Yes, I think so.
T: Well, I think we'll leave it at that.

In this dialogue there is no IRF structure. The pupils not only
initiate exchanges, but question the teacher's interpretation of
what they have said. This is rather more what we mean by
genuine discussion. And it implies quite different concepts of
knowledge, and a different concept of teacher and pupil roles.
Again, note how this approach to classroom knowledge shows
the impossibility of separating cognitive and social aspects of
learning.

7.4 The social construction of children's ability

It is not only knowledge which is (partly) defined through
teacher–pupil interaction. A pupil's *ability* must be constructed
and defined through classroom dialogue.

Hammersley (1974) discusses how it comes about that some
pupils are judged 'intelligent' by teachers. He points out that
such judgements are made on the basis of pupils' behaviour,
particularly their ability to answer teachers' questions correctly.
That is, such classifications of pupils are made (partly) on the
basis of their communicative competence in participating in
classroom discourse. In the kind of formal chalk-and-talk classrooms Hammersley studied, pupils have to demonstrate intelligence by getting the teacher to hear their answers and accept
them as 'correct'. In order to do this, they must recognize the
teacher's sole right to organize classroom interaction, to choose
topics of discussion, and to demand and evaluate their answers.
Pupils who challenge these rights are liable to have their answers
ignored. The teacher might say, for example, 'Don't shout out!'

Answers must be appropriately presented in order to be acceptable.

Mehan (1973) takes this idea further by showing how a child's 'ability' is not an absolute quality, but the outcome of a social encounter: the 'test'. Test results are often regarded as the product of a passive, standardized, routine record made objectively (mechanically?) by the tester. But such results, and therefore the child's IQ, are rather the outcome of how the child *interprets* the questions and how the tester *interprets* the answers. Thus one question in a language-development test instructs the child to choose the 'animal that can fly', from a bird, an elephant and a dog. Many young children choose the elephant along with the bird. If they are asked why, they explain 'That's Dumbo', i.e. Walt Disney's flying elephant. A 'wrong' answer here does not therefore indicate a *lack* of ability, but an *alternative* interpretive schema: in this case they are not separating what adults would regard as reality and fantasy.

We have already seen (Ch. 6.4) that the social relations in the classroom or test can crucially affect estimates of children's linguistic capacity. Now, we see also that the test is itself a communicative encounter, a social dialogue of questions and answers, which can itself be studied as discourse. Children do not 'possess' an IQ: their ability is constructed by the very social situation in which it is measured. It is thus through the organization of teacher–pupil or tester–pupil dialogue that children's ability comes to be constructed by teachers and testers. Pupils are judged bright or dim according to whether they interact appropriately, and as adults expect, in particular sociolinguistic situations. Much work has now shown how children's performance may differ radically in different social situations. (See Labov, 1969, discussed in Ch. 4.3; Philips, 1972; and Dumont, 1972, discussed below.)

7.5 Teaching as talking: some cross-cultural data

Consider, finally, some broader ways of thinking about what educational assumptions and conceptions of knowledge underlie classroom language. Many educationalists have put forward versions of the view that pupils learn through talking. One often comes across statements such as:

> Not only do we learn by doing, but we also learn by talking about an experience. . . . Our pupils will learn most by reading, writing and talking about the experiences they meet and through this will in time come to terms with subject disciplines. (Barnes *et al.*, 1969, p. 126)

Many teachers certainly hold the view that pupils learn by expressing things in their own words. This is why we distrust a pupil's work if he or she has simply copied it from a book. Flanders (1970) takes it for granted that it is a good thing if pupils can be encouraged simply to talk *more* in lessons. Clearly he is interested in quality as well as quantity, but simply a larger amount of pupil-talk is assumed to be a good thing. Much of my discussion of teacher–pupil dialogue has centred on the fact that teachers are often concerned to elicit talk from pupils, to get them to answer questions at appropriate moments.

Consider this teacher with a class of 12 year olds:

> T: David, about time I heard your voice this morning – so wake up, it's not very difficult this, for even you. Come on, David, show some sparks of life.
> P: (Answers question)
> T: What? Pardon? Well, speak up, don't speak to your hand, your hand is not very interested in this – we are . . .

This teacher is making fairly explicit some of his assumptions about the place of language in the classroom: that it is a good thing just to 'hear a pupil's voice'; and that public talk should be the norm. This teacher clearly assumed that an important part of learning is a public, verbal display of knowledge. Often, we tend to evaluate teachers according to how freely they can 'get pupils to talk'.

One might question the view that it is a good thing if a pupil is merely standing on his feet, composing talk in real time in front of an audience. Some control over style and content is necessary

130

at some point. But there is a prima-facie case, if only from common experience, that one can clarify ideas by 'talking them through' and defending them in dialogue with others. There are, of course, things that have to be demonstrated or practised in order to be learned. A pupil cannot demonstrate knowledge of technical drawing just by talking about it. But, in general, schools are particularly concerned with publicly communicable types of knowledge, and, in the past at least, 'education' has often been equated with literacy.

Note, however, that this view of education is *culture specific*. That is, this equation of learning with talking is widely held in our society, but is by no means universal. Philips (1972) and Dumont (1972) discuss the problem of the 'silent' 'American Indian child. Both authors start from the frequent complaint of White teachers with classes of Indian children that their pupils 'won't talk' in class – although they are observed to be highly verbal in other social situations. They both explain this by showing how the Indian groups in question (Cherokee and Sioux) have quite different sociolinguistic norms and values concerning the use of speech. In particular, Philips shows that the Indian groups believe that learning occurs through observation, supervised participation and self-initiated testing. Speech is minimal in this process.

Such ethnographic data from different cultures shows up our society's taken-for-granted equation of language, written or spoken, as the primary channel through which educational knowledge should be transmitted. This is not a necessary or natural feature of learning. Our society values highly the role of language in education and tends therefore to assume that children with radically different language from their teachers are cognitively different, or even cognitively deficient (see Ch. 4).

In summary: very general sociolinguistic norms may be conveyed by the fine grain and overall structure of classroom dialogue. Teachers who ask sequences of closed questions, or university lecturers who talk for 50 minutes without stopping, or teachers who try to get pupils to talk more, are all displaying

131

in the form and structure of their talk implicit theories of the relation of teaching and learning to language, and of what it means for students to be 'intelligent'.

The study of classroom language thus brings out very clearly that the act of teaching is culturally defined. *Teaching IS sociolinguistic behaviour*, and by studying it as such one can recover some of the educators' assumptions which underlie it. Different levels of meaning in this chapter's title, 'Teaching and talking', should now be evident. On the one hand, teacher–pupil talk is just talk and is open to sociolinguistic description as any other type of discourse is. But also, our culture assumes that teaching and learning are somehow necessarily dependent on language. This culture-bound assumption about the role of language in education is, in turn, revealed in the underlying discourse structure of the classroom talk itself.

8

Towards a sociolinguistic analysis of language in education

Throughout, we have seen the complexities of the relationships between language and the social contexts in which it is used, and we have therefore seen that any simple causal model purporting to relate *superficial* aspects of language *directly* to educational processes will be oversimple. 'Superficial' aspects of language include accent, grammatical differences between standard and nonstandard dialects, the proportion of grammatically complex sentences a speaker uses, and so on. There is no evidence whatsoever that such features of language are related, for example, to thought processes. We have also seen that certain concepts (such as restricted code and verbal deprivation), which are being taken for granted by many educationalists and psychologists, are being seriously questioned by linguists as having little or no basis in linguistic fact. We must therefore now try to reach some conclusions about the state of research in this area, and about what would constitute a sociolinguistically adequate statement of the role of language in education. These will be tentative conclusions, it is only since around 1970 that any concentrated amount of work has been done on the role of language in education. Much of the work has been done by psychologists and sociologists, and only comparatively recently have linguists begun to show an interest: Hymes (e.g. 1972) and Labov have led the way here.

Certain principles do, however, seem clear. I have argued that an adequate analysis of language in education must be based at least partly on (a) a close analysis of real language, observed and recorded as far as possible in natural social situations, especially in the classroom itself; and (b) adequate sociolinguistic concepts to handle the complex relations between language, attitudes to language and the social contexts of language use. We require also (c) a systematic framework which describes the languages in use in the wider community beyond the school and in the country as a whole. In Britain, this means different accents and dialects of English, whether native to Britain (for example, Cockney) or spoken here due to recent immigration (for example, Caribbean creoles); and also languages other than English, whether native to Britain (for example, Welsh) or spoken here due to recent immigration (for example, Punjabi). A full discussion of this aspect of language diversity is beyond the scope of this book, but is discussed in more detail in the companion reader.

8.1 Language as evidence for educational statements

The work discussed in this book comprises attempts, in one way or another, to use aspects of language as *evidence for educational statements*. That is, aspects of children's or teachers' language are recorded or observed, and these linguistic data are used as 'indicators', 'markers' or 'indices' of learning and teaching processes. Sometimes, aspects of language are said, further, to be the causes of educational phenomena, for example the determinants of teachers' effectiveness or pupils' educability. It is revealing to consider just *what is related to what* in such statements.

It becomes clear, first, that different studies take language as evidence of a very mixed collection of educational processes, including: the cognitive orientation of pupils; possible barriers to pupils' learning and understanding; teaching strategies, e.g. 'open' versus 'closed'; methods of social control in the classroom; different types of classroom organization, e.g. 'formal' versus 'informal'; taken-for-granted concepts of classroom knowledge. This list could be extended.

Second, different studies pick out a very mixed collection of linguistic items as 'indicators' of such educational concepts, including: teachers' differing use of pronouns (e.g. Mishler, 1972; Torode, 1976); the complexity of noun groups (cf. Ch. 3.2); intonation and paralinguistic clues (cf. Ch. 6.1); the overall structure of teaching cycles (cf. Ch. 6.2). This list could also be extended. In general, different researchers seem to feel justified in selecting as evidence any feature of language which strikes their intuition as interesting. More particularly, the linguistic items are selected, apparently, according to the whim of the researcher, from different levels of language, including lexis (i.e. individual words), syntax (i.e. grammatical structure), semantics (i.e. meaning) and discourse (i.e. overall conversational structure).

Such linguistic items are then often related *directly* to educational statements. Together, then, these points mean that studies of language in education often attempt to relate concepts which are at quite incompatible levels of abstraction and generality. Often isolated, surface features of language (e.g. use of pronouns or frequency of complex noun groups) are taken as indicators of highly abstract educational concepts (e.g. 'open' teaching style or educability). Many studies of classrooms, for example, characteristically *select* for quotation short *extracts* of recorded classroom talk, and *select* particular features of the extract as *evidence* for some nonlinguistic statements. It is often assumed that details of what teachers and pupils say can serve unproblematically as illustrations of the educational process. Thus readers may be expected to be able to recognize a particular teacher–pupil interchange as an instance of, say, a 'democratic' teacher or of a pupil who is 'thinking for himself'. But such

135

claimed relationships, between surface features of language and educational concepts, may lack any principled basis.

8.2 Language is organized

On the face of it, there is no reason why superficial or isolated linguistic items should be interpretable as direct evidence of educational processes. For example, the cognitive complexity of an argument can never be computed directly by calculating the average length of its sentences, or by counting the number of subordinate clauses, rare adjectives or complex noun groups it contains. Such crude linguistic measures have been used in some studies as indices of cognitive variables, and such studies have been cited above. But it should be clear that there is no necessary connection between complex or unusual linguistic structures and complex cognitive processes. Profound arguments may be stated in simple language, and trivial thoughts may be dressed up in superficially complex language.

The relation between language and social or cognitive processes is much less direct than this – and much more interesting.

Consider, for example, the type of relationship which sociolinguists have found between language and social structure. Labov's work can provide a precise example. In a major article, Labov (1973) studies the language of pre-adolescent Negro gangs in Harlem. He found the boys' language to be a sensitive *index* of how closely the boys were involved in the street culture. That is, he identified core members and marginal members ('lames') of the gangs by nonlinguistic methods. He then found that the language of the core members differed systematically from the lames' language. But the important point is that their language did not differ in the use of particular words or isolated items. What differed was the *whole system*. Labov's finding was that the core members' language was more consistent in its use of the rules of BEV. The index of street culture is therefore provided by the overall consistency of the whole linguistic system.

The main point is that if language is to be used as evidence of social structure and processes, then it must be examined *as a system*, not as isolated items. Since relations are found between linguistic systems and social structures, the language data must be studied for their own systematic linguistic organization.

Another way of phrasing the criticism of the last section is therefore to say that language is often used as data for educational statements *as though the language had no organization of its own*. However, one of the fundamental principles of this book has been that we will never fully understand the role of language in education unless we take into account *how language itself works*. Linguistics treats language as a highly organized phenomenon, tightly structured and patterned at many levels, including the levels of sound, word structure, meaning, sentence structure, discourse and social context.

The principle of treating language as an organized system has been illustrated in several ways. Detailed examples were given above of why standard and nonstandard dialects must both be treated as systematic wholes, with their own internal organization. It is quite misleading, and counter to all the linguistic evidence, to treat nonstandard dialects as erratic deviations from the standard language: they are highly organized systems in their own right (see Ch. 4.1). It is similarly misleading to treat spoken language as a series of isolated utterances, rather than as connected discourse. My criticism of Hawkins's experiment (Ch. 3.2) was that he failed to take account of the conversational organization of his data, but tried instead to relate isolated linguistic items (frequency of noun groups) directly to the cognitive orientation of children. That is, Hawkins proposed a cognitive explanation of his data, whereas I would propose a sociolinguistic explanation, as Hawkins (1977) himself does in later work.

As an example of the need to treat language in terms of its discourse organization, and not as single, isolated utterances, we might return to the question of assessing children's verbal capacity. A book on Bernstein's theories (Lee, 1973) has the following cover design:

Q: What is a dog?
A: A dog is furry and barks.
Restricted code? Elaborated code?

(This exchange is shown against a photograph of a little boy who is looking studiously at a book.)

Q: What is a dog?
A: You have a dog at home.
Restricted code? Elaborated code?

(This exchange is shown against a photograph of another little boy, who somehow looks rather scruffier, and who is gazing at nothing in particular, turned round in his chair.)

This is hypothetical data, of the crude kind rejected earlier, comprising the cover design of a book; but for that reason it catches the attention and is worth comment. In this area, it is often the crude stereotyping of linguistic behaviour which does damage. I take it the implication is that answer (1) is elaborated code, because it is an *ex*plicit definition; and that answer (2) is restricted code, because it is *im*plicit and would not define a dog for someone who had no idea what a dog was. On the other hand, regarded as *discourse*, exchange (1) is rather odd and stilted. Whereas exchange (2) shows the kind of oblique answer to questions which commonly occurs in normal conversation. Answer (2) would, in many circumstances, be a more helpful type of answer: it is the kind of answer which refuses, sensibly, to assume that the questioner really has no idea what a dog is, and thus refuses to treat discourse as an artificial game. The moral is that utterances have to be seen *within their system* of discourse, and not as isolated events. And in general therefore, linguistic items have to be related to linguistic systems before being used as evidence for cognitive or sociological statements.

A well-known analogy for this point in linguistics is as follows. Suppose you want to analyse the meaning of a move in a game of chess. It would be pointless to try and explain a move by *direct* reference to the intelligence of the players, or other such factors. The point of a particular move can only be understood by relating it both to the state of play on the board and also, of course, to the rules of chess. For someone observing a game of chess with no knowledge of the rules, any isolated move would literally have no meaning at all. A move only has meaning within the system of the game, and has no absolute value in itself. This analogy holds for any game. In card games as a whole, the five of spades, say, has no meaning. Its value depends (a) on the particular game being played; and (b) on what context it occurs in within the game, e.g. along with three other fives, or in a run of spades. It is similarly misleading if a literary critic tries to relate an incident in a novel directly to, say, the social context in which the book was written; an event in the author's childhood; or some underlying characteristic of the author's personality. An incident in a novel must first be understood in relation to the structure of the novel as a whole: it might, after all, be required simply to advance the plot one stage.

Such analogies could be multiplied. Although analogies can be misleading if pushed too far, they are often helpful in grasping a concept. In a book of this sort, it is possible only to suggest a couple of analogies to the reader and to refer back to the previous discussion of the ways in which language is organized at the levels of dialect (Ch. 2.2 and 4.1), discourse (Chs 6.2 and 7.3) and grammar (Ch. 2.4).

It is, then, only sensible to try and account for bits of language in terms of linguistic systems wherever possible, before proceeding to non-linguistic explanations. Again, this has been a general, but so far largely implicit, principle in the present book. One of the general arguments throughout has been that it is more plausible to account for the effect of language on educational success in terms of people's attitudes to language, rather than to propose that different language varieties have different cognitive effects. That is, I have constantly proposed a sociolinguistic account of language in education, rather than make direct links between language and cognitive ability. Language and thought are related in some way, but no one has yet shown precisely what this link is, and it is demonstrably *not* a simple, causal link. Similarly, one can account for the poor

139

performance of many children in classroom or test situations by pointing to precise sociolinguistic constraints on such occasions. Again, one can propose a sociolinguistic explanation of differences in language use between different social groups, without resorting to the assumption that one group is cognitively inferior to the other.

The general theoretical point at issue here can be summarized as follows. When we are dealing with linguistic data (audio-recordings, fieldnotes, language elicited in tests and so on) we must study how linguistic items are related in linguistic and sociolinguistic systems (e.g. within dialects, in connected discourse and in norms of usage in different social contexts). It is not sufficient to relate linguistic items directly to non-linguistic (e.g. cognitive, educational, sociological) categories. They must first be related to the linguistic and sociolinguistic systems in which they are terms.

8.3 Criteria for studies of language in education

The demands which one has to make for work on language in education are therefore as follows. The work should be based primarily on *naturalistic observation* and recording of language in real social situations: mainly in the classroom itself, but also in the home, and in the peer group, which is the most powerful linguistic influence on children. The work must be based on a linguistically adequate analysis of what is said. This means both being *explicit* about the relation between language forms and functions and also analysing language as *linguistic systems*. It is not enough, however, for the analysis to be rigorous in a mechanical way: what is required is an analysis of the *social meanings* conveyed by language and an analysis of people's *attitudes* to language. Finally, if we are to understand the general principles underlying the sociolinguistic forces at work in schools, the analysis of language in educational settings must be related to what we know of sociolinguistic behaviour in other settings.

These demands are stringent, and it will be clear to the reader that no work, including the present book, yet satisfies them on all counts. Much work fails, however, to meet any of the demands, while other work meets some of the criteria. And the demands must be made if we are to progress beyond linguistic folklore, personal opinions, unsupported speculation, pseudo-theories and an accumulation of interesting anecdotes; none of which, in themselves, can lead to real understanding.

9

Some topics for investigation

This book has tried to provide the reader with the basic concepts necessary to understand the continuing debate over the place of language in education. Most importantly, perhaps, it has tried to illustrate how various researchers have begun to investigate how language is used in schools and classrooms. Rather than summarize the argument, I will devote this last chapter to listing some topics which readers could now go on to study for themselves. Suggesting topics for investigation will also point to many aspects of language which this book has not dealt with, largely because we know very little about them.

There is no reason at all why student teachers, for example, should not investigate, possibly in a quite informal way, one of the topics suggested below. Students on teaching practice often have to spend considerable periods of time just 'observing'. What this means depends very much on the school they find themselves in. But students often find themselves sitting in classrooms, unsure of what or how to 'observe'. Yet armed with a few ideas, a notebook and possibly a tape-recorder (if teachers and pupils have no objection to being recorded) the observation period can be exciting and informative. So here are several topics on which readers could collect badly needed information.

Different types of classroom language

We still know very little about *what actually happens in class-rooms*, between teachers and pupils, and have little basic descriptive information about teacher-pupil dialogue in different teaching situations. The extracts of teacher–pupil talk in this book have been drawn from a very narrow range of class-rooms, largely from rather formal chalk-and-talk lessons. Readers of this book will have experience of many types of teaching which have not even been touched on. We lack basic descriptive information about the kinds of teacher–pupil interaction in small rural schools, in bilingual classrooms in Wales, in open-plan Nuffield science lessons, in remedial reading classes, in team-teaching sessions and so on. Primarily, we need to be able to relate generalizations about language in education to a wide range of observational data on different types of classrooms. The most important research will certainly be done in the classroom, and such information can be provided only by observers in the classroom. Walker and Adelman (1975a) provide excellent practical advice on doing such observation.

Learning the rules of classroom discourse

Chapters 6 and 7 discuss the expectations which teachers and pupils have about appropriate classroom discourse. But little is known about how children learn the rules of the verbal game. Classroom discourse is characteristically different from other discourse types, and somehow children must learn the sociolinguistic behaviour expected of them. Some children may learn one type of classroom game from their mothers (see Ch. 7.2). Other rules may be taught explicitly by teachers who tell children, 'Don't shout out!', 'Don't all talk at once' or 'Put your hand up before your answer'. Much information could be

143

collected on this by observing playgroups, or in particular, the first few days a child spends at primary school or at a new school or with a new teacher. Willes (in press) provides a model for such a study.

The language environment of a lesson

The total language environment of a lesson consists only partly of the teacher–pupil dialogue, although in most lessons this is likely to be the major part. It consists also of textbooks, worksheets, handouts, charts or posters on the wall, whatever the teacher writes on the board, pupils' writing, and possibly radio programmes or films. As well as recording public talk, it might be possible to collect copies of worksheets or similar material; to xerox relevant pages of books or pupils' own writing; to copy down blackboard notes or to photograph them along with relevant wallcharts. It may also be possible to collect observations on pupil–pupil talk in lessons. Often this is not public and is consequently difficult to observe, but a great deal is possible by informal observation.

In this way, one might try to construct, as far as practically possible, the total language environment of a single lesson. When such material has been collected, it can be compared in various ways, to study, for example, how written and spoken materials on the same topics differ in style and in the linguistic demands made on pupils.

The uses of written material

Part of the language environment of a classroom is written material. However, it is rare to find observational studies of how pupils actually use books, worksheets, wallcharts, notes on the blackboard, and so on. How much of their time is spent reading and writing? Do they read aloud or silently? Do they discuss written material with a neighbour or in groups? Do they learn it by heart or rewrite it in their own words? In reading a book, do they start at page one and keep going, or do they use the contents page and index to move around in the book to find what they are immediately interested in? Do such reading strategies differ with different kinds of books, for example fiction versus non-fiction? Do they use reference books such as dictionaries and encyclopedias? Lunzer and Gardner (1978) discuss many such issues.

The language environment of a school

Alternatively, one could collect examples of the range of different kinds of language used throughout a school. What kind of hidden curriculum is conveyed, for example, by the language in different textbooks? the language of the school rules? the language of morning assembly or prize day? the language of the school motto? the language of the school or class magazine? the language of examination papers? and so on.

The term 'language climate' is sometimes used to describe the very different kinds of linguistic demands made on pupils by such uses of language. Often this term implies a vague and woolly horticultural theory of education: that learning 'thrives' best in a favourable 'climate'. But it is possible to specify precisely what constitutes such a climate by collecting specimens of language and considering just what implicit messages they convey.

Child–child talk

Although the most important research will be done in classrooms, we also require descriptions of *how children talk to other children when no adults are present.* For it is a well-documented sociolinguistic fact that a child's friends are a more powerful influence on his or her language than both family and school. Almost all the research on children's sociolinguistic behaviour has focused on adult–child talk, usually mother–child or teacher–pupil. We know very little about how children talk, in the playground or outside school, when no adults are around.

145

Clearly there is a paradox in trying to observe how children interact when the adult observer is not present. But a lot is possible by informal observation of snatches of conversation caught in passing, or by tape-recording groups of children (with their permission!) when no adult is in the room. The pressure of normal social contacts with friends will often outweigh, at least partly, the presence of the tape-recorder. Labov (1973) provides an important technical study of the powerful influence of gang membership on children's language.

A good way to collect data on children's language is to take advantage of any opportunities which arise to observe children when they gather together in places with no adults in control: in adventure playgrounds, at school bus-stops, and the like. If it is possible to observe children without attracting their attention, good data can be collected informally on how they interact amongst themselves. The conversational rules are very different from adult–child or adult–adult dialogue! McTear (1981) provides interesting analysis of conversation between two young children.

The languages used in a school

In multilingual classrooms it might be possible to investigate which languages children know. This would have to be approached very carefully and tactfully, since such questions will almost inevitably raise social and ethnic attitudes, and whilst some children may be proud of their knowledge of different languages, others may well be ashamed of what they think are 'not real languages' or what they know well are low-prestige varieties. The questions rapidly become complex. Just what is meant by knowing a language? Can languages just be counted? Do children have a passive understanding of a language other than English, or do they actively use it at home? Do they use it only with particular groups of people? Do they read and write it as well as speak it? Does the language have particular cultural or religious functions? Rosen and Burgess (1980) discuss both the difficulties in defining what is meant by

Further reading

1 Companion reader

Michael Stubbs and Hilary Hillier (eds) (1983) *Readings on Language, Schools and Classrooms*. London: Methuen.
This contains articles on topics discussed here, such as classroom language and Caribbean creoles, and also articles on other topics only mentioned briefly here if at all: for example, accents and dialects of British English, ethnic-minority languages in Britain, reading and writing, and listening comprehension.

2 General and introductory books on linguistics in education
(Particularly relevant to Chapter 1)

David Crystal (1976) *Child Language, Learning and Linguistics: an Overview for the Teaching and Therapeutic Professions*. London: Edward Arnold.
An accurate title.

Ronald Carter (ed.) (1982) *Linguistics and the Teacher*. London: Routledge & Kegan Paul.
Ten articles on the value of linguistics to teachers, making precise proposals about the place of linguistics in both teacher training and in the classroom.

149

3 The sociolinguistic perspective
(Particularly relevant to Chapters 2, 3 and 4)

Gordon, J. C. B. (1981) *Verbal Deficit: a Critique*. London: Croom Helm.
A short, clear book on verbal deficit theories in general, and Bernstein's work in particular.

William Labov (1969) The logic of nonstandard English. In *Language in the Inner City*. Oxford: Blackwell, 1977 (and reprinted in many other places).
A very important and influential article: highly recommended.

Michael Stubbs (1980) *Language and Literacy: the Sociolinguistics of Reading and Writing*. London: Routledge & Kegan Paul.
A discussion of the relations between spoken and written language, including spelling and the different functions of speech and writing.

Peter Trudgill (1975) *Accent, Dialect and the School*. London: Edward Arnold.
Short and precise. Very much influenced by Labov's work. Argues that accent and dialect cause educational problems only because of people's intolerance of linguistic diversity.

4 Classroom language
(Particularly relevant to Chapters 5, 6 and 7)

Douglas Barnes *et al.* (1969, revised ed. 1971) *Language, the Learner and the School*. Harmondsworth: Penguin.
Informal and discursive, but well illustrated by many examples of classroom talk. A very influential study.

Sara Delamont (1976, revised ed. 1983) *Interaction in the Classroom*. London: Methuen.
In the same series as the present book. A short introduction to a sociological theory of classrooms and teacher–pupil interaction. Complementary to the present book since it covers some of the same topics from a different theoretical position.

Michael Stubbs and Sara Delamont (eds) (1976) *Explorations in Classroom Observation*. London: Wiley.
A collection of articles on classroom behaviour, all based on direct observation and recording in real classrooms.

Mary Willes (in press) *Children into Pupils: a Study of Language in Early Schooling*. London: Routledge & Kegan Paul.
A very readable observational account of children's first days and weeks in school. Based on Sinclair and Coulthard's work (see Ch. 6.2).

References and
name index

The numbers in italics after each entry refer to page numbers within this book.

Atkinson, P. (1975) In cold blood: bedside teaching in a medical school. In Chanan and Delamont (eds). *107, 126*

Atkinson, P. (1981) Bernstein's structuralism. *Educational Analysis*, 3, 1. *66*

Barnes, D. (1969) Language in the secondary classroom. In Barnes *et al*. *100-3, 106, 114, 120, 124, 130, 150*

Barnes, D. (1971) Language and learning in the classroom. *Journal of Curriculum Studies 3*, I. *101*

Barnes, D., Britton, J. and Rosen, H. (1969, revised ed. 1971) *Language, the Learner and the School*. Harmondsworth: Penguin.

Barnes, D. and Todd, F. (1977) *Communication and Learning in Small Groups*. London: Routledge & Kegan Paul. *116*

Bellack, A. (ed.) (1973) *Studies in the Classroom Language*. New York: Teachers College Press. *114*

Bellack, A. A., Kliebard, H. M., Hyman, R. T. and Smith, F. L. (1966) *The Language of the Classroom*. New York: Teachers College Press. *107-8*

Bernstein, B. (ed.) (1971a, 1972, 1973, 1975) *Class, Codes and Control*, vols. 1, 2 and 3. London: Routledge & Kegan Paul (references to vol. 1 in the text are to the revised ed. of vol. 1, 1973, London: Paladin). *47–50, 55–9, 62, 64–6, 79, 121-3*

Bernstein, B. (1971b) On the classification and framing of educational knowledge. In Young (ed.) (1971). *122–3*

Boggs, S. T. (1972) The meaning of questions and narratives to Hawaian children. In Cazden *et al.* (eds). *77*

Burton, D. (1980) *Dialogue and Discourse.* London: Routledge & Kegan Paul. *111*

Cazden, C., John, V., Hymes, D. (eds) (1972) *Functions of Language in the Classroom.* New York: Teachers College Press.

Chanan, G. and Delamont, S. (eds) (1975) *Frontiers of Classroom Research.* Slough: NFER.

Cheshire, J. (1982) *Variation in an English Dialect.* Cambridge: Cambridge University Press. *12*

Creber, P. (1972) *Lost for Words.* Harmondsworth: Penguin. *85*

Crystal, D. (1976) *Child Language, Learning and Linguistics: an Overview for the Teaching and Therapeutic Professions.* London: Edward Arnold. *23, 149*

Crystal, D. (1980) *Introduction to Language Pathology.* London: Edward Arnold. *12*

Delamont, S. (1976, revised ed. 1983) *Interaction in the Classroom.* London: Methuen. *92, 93, 124, 150*

Delamont, S. (1983) *Readings on Interaction in the Classroom.* London: Methuen.

Delamont, S. and Hamilton, D. (1976) Classroom research: a critique and a new approach. In Stubbs and Delamont (eds). *92, 94*

Dittmar, N. (1976) *Sociolinguistics.* London: Edward Arnold. *65*

Dumont, R. V. (1972) Learning English and how to be silent: studies in Sioux and Cherokee classrooms. In Cazden *et al.* (eds). *77, 129, 131*

Edwards, J. R. (1979) *Language and Disadvantage.* London: Edward Arnold. *65*

Edwards, V. K. (1979) *The West Indian Language Issue in British Schools.* London: Routledge & Kegan Paul. *12, 68, 82*

Flanders, N. (1970) *Analysing Teaching Behaviour.* London: Addison-Wesley. *17, 130*

Flower, F. D. (1966) *Language and Education.* London: Longman. *85*

French, P. and MacLure, M. (eds) (1981) *Adult–Child Conversation.* London: Croom Helm. *111*

Furlong, V. (1976) Interaction sets in the classroom: towards a study of pupil knowledge. In Stubbs and Delamont (eds). *124*

Gannaway, H. (1976) Making sense of school. In Stubbs and Delamont (eds). *124*

Gazdar, G. (1979) Class, 'codes' and conversation. *Linguistics*, 17. *56*

Giles, H. (1971) Our reactions to accent. *New Society*, 14 October. *26*

Gordon, J. C. B. (1981) *Verbal Deficit: A Critique*. London: Croom Helm. *60, 65, 150*

Greene, J. (1975) *Thinking and Language*. London: Methuen. *19*

Gumperz, J. J. and Herasimchuk, E. (1972) The conversational analysis of social meaning: a study of classroom interaction. In R. Shuy (ed.) *Sociolinguistics*. Georgetown Monograph Series on Language and Linguistics, 25. *105*

Hall, R. A. Jr (1972) Pidgins and creoles as standard languages. In Pride and Holmes (eds). *72*

Hamilton, D. (1976) The advent of curriculum integration: paradigm lost or paradigm regained? In Stubbs and Delamont (eds). *119*

Hammersley, M. (1974) The organization of pupil participation. *Sociological Review 22*, 3, 355–68. *128*

Hawkins, P. (1969) Social class, the nominal group and reference. In Bernstein (ed.) (1972). *50–3, 137*

Hawkins, P. (1977) *Social Class, the Nominal Group and Verbal Strategies*. London: Routledge & Kegan Paul. *53–4, 137*

Herriot, P. (1971) *Language and Teaching*. London: Methuen. *85*

Hess, R. D. and Shipman, V. C. (1965) Early experience and the socialization of cognitive modes in children. In A. Cashdan and E. Grudgeon (eds) (1972) *Language in Education*. London: Routledge & Kegan Paul. *74–6*

HMSO (1975) *A Language for Life*. Report of the Bullock Committee. London: HMSO. *11, 21–3, 84*

HMSO (1981) *West Indian Children in Our Schools*. Interim Report of the Rampton Committee of Inquiry into the Education of Children from Ethnic Minority Groups. London: HMSO. *83–4*

Hoetker, J. and Ahlbrandt, P. A. (1969) The persistence of recitation. *American Educational Research Journal 6*, 2. *114*

Hughes, A. and Trudgill, P. (1979) *English Accents and Dialects*. London: Edward Arnold. *12, 37*

Hymes, D. (1967) Models of the interaction of language and social setting. *Journal of Social Issues 23*, 2. *39*

Hymes, D. (1972) Introduction. In Cazden *et al.* (eds). *29, 95, 97, 134*

Jackson, L. A. (1974) The myth of elaborated and restricted code. *Higher Education Review 6*, 2. *62, 65, 85*

Jackson, P. W. (1968) *Life in Classrooms*. New York: Holt, Rinehart & Winston. *93, 119–20*

Keddie, N. (1971) Classroom knowledge. In Young (ed.). *18, 124*

Keddie, N. (ed.) (1973) *Tinker, Tailor . . . The Myth of Cultural Deprivation*, Harmondsworth: Penguin. *85*

Kochman, T. (1972) Black American speech events and a language programme for the classrooms. In Cazden *et al. 62, 74*

Labov, W. (1969) *The Logic of Nonstandard English*. Washington, DC: Center for Applied Linguistics. (Also in Keddie (ed.) and Labov (1972a). *43, 62, 65, 68–71, 76, 79, 85, 116, 129, 150*

Labov, W. (1970) The study of language in its social context. Excerpt in Pride and Holmes (eds). In Labov, 1972b. *79*

Labov, W. (1972a) *Language in the Inner City*. Philadelphia: University of Pennsylvania Press. (Also published in 1977 by Blackwell, Oxford.) *67, 74, 94, 147*

Labov, W. (1972b) *Sociolinguistic Patterns*. Philadelphia: University of Pennsylvania Press. (Also published in 1977 by Blackwell, Oxford.) *39, 67, 148*

Labov, W. (1973) The linguistic consequences of being a lame. *Language in Society 2*, 1. *136, 146*

Lambert, W. E. (1967) A social psychology of bilingualism. In Pride and Holmes (eds). *73*

Lee, V. (1973) *Social Relationships and Language*. Milton Keynes: Open University Press. *137–8*

Le Page, R. B. (1981) *Caribbean Connections in the Classroom*. London: Mary Glasgow Trust. Extract in Stubbs and Hillier (eds). *12, 150*

Lunzer, E. A. and Gardner, K. (eds) (1978) *The Effective Use of Reading*. London: Heinemann. *12, 145*

Macaulay, R. K. S. (1978) *Language, Social Class and Education: a Glasgow Study*. Edinburgh: University Press. *12, 28, 41, 67, 71, 73, 86*

McTear, M. F. (1981) Towards a model for analysing conversations involving children. In French and MacLure (eds). *146*

Medley, D. M. and Mitzel, H. E. (1963) Measuring classroom behaviour by systematic observation. In N. L. Gage (ed.) *Handbook of Research on Teaching*. Chicago: Rand McNally. *92*

Mehan, H. (1973) Assessing children's school performance. In H. P. Dreitzel (ed.) *Children and Socialization*, Recent Sociology 5. London: Macmillan. *129*

Mehrabian, A. (1968) Inference of attitudes from the posture, orientation and distance of a communicator. In M. Argyle (ed.) (1973) *Social Encounters*. Harmondsworth: Penguin. *95*

Milroy, L. (1980) *Language and Social Networks*. Oxford: Blackwell. *12, 67*

Milroy, L. and Milroy, J. (in prep.) *Authority in Language: a Socio-linguistic Analysis of Prescriptivism*. London: Routledge & Kegan Paul. *28, 147*

Milroy, J. and Milroy, L. (1974) A sociolinguistic project in Belfast. Queen's University, Belfast, mimeo. *28*

Mishler, E. (1972) Implications of teacher-strategies for language and cognition: observations in first-grade classrooms. In Cazden *et al.* (eds). *103–4, 135*

Mitchell-Kernan, C. (1972) On the status of Black English for native speakers: an assessment of attitudes and values. In Cazden *et al.* (eds). *73*

Mittins, W. H. (1969) What is correctness? *Educational Review 22*, 1. *42*

Nuthall, G. A. (1968) A review of some selected recent studies of classroom interaction and teaching behaviour. In J. Gallagher *et al. Classroom Observation*. Chicago: Rand McNally. *92*

Philips, S. (1972) Participant structures and communicative competence: Warm Springs children in community and classroom. In Cazden *et al.* (eds). *77, 129, 131*

Postman, N. and Weingartner, C. (1969) *Teaching as a Subversive Activity*. New York: Delacorte. (Also published in 1971 by Penguin: Harmondsworth.) *90, 114*

Pride, J. and Holmes, J. (eds) (1972) *Sociolinguistics*. Harmondsworth: Penguin.

Rosen, H. (1973) *Language and Class: A Critical Look at the Theories of Basil Bernstein*. Bristol: Falling Wall Press. *65*

Rosen, H. and Burgess, R. (1980) *Languages and Dialects of London Schoolchildren*. London: Ward Lock. *12, 146*

Rosenthal, R. and Jacobson, L. (1968) *Pygmalion in the Classroom*. New York: Holt, Rinehart & Winston. *84*

Seligman, C. R., Tucker, G. R. and Lambert, W. E. (1972) The effects of speech style and other attributes on teachers' attitudes towards children. *Language in Society 1*, 1. *26*

Sharp, D. (1973) *Language in Bilingual Communities*. London: Edward Arnold. *29*

Simon, A. and Boyer, E. B. (eds) (1967, 1970) *Mirrors for Behaviour*. Philadelphia: Research for Better Schools. *92*

Sinclair, J. M. (1973) English for effect. *Commonwealth Education Liaison Committee Newsletter 3*, 11. *80, 82*

Sinclair, J. M. and Coulthard, R. M. (1975) *Towards an Analysis of Discourse: The English Used by Teachers and Pupils*. Oxford: Oxford University Press. *108–11, 124–5*

Snyder, B. (1971) *The Hidden Curriculum*. New York: Knopf. *119*

Stubbs, M. (1975) Teaching and talking: a sociolinguistic approach to classroom interaction. In Chanan and Delamont (eds).

Stubbs, M. (1976) Keeping in touch: some functions of teacher-talk. In Stubbs and Delamont (eds). *105–6*

Stubbs, M. (1980) *Language and Literacy: the Sociolinguistics of Reading and Writing*. London: Routledge & Kegan Paul. *13, 31, 37, 65, 73, 150*

Stubbs, M. (1983) *Discourse Analysis*. Oxford: Blackwell. *111*

Stubbs, M. and Delamont, S. (eds) (1976) *Explorations in Classroom Observation*. London: Wiley. *93, 150*

Stubbs, M. and Hillier, H. (eds) (1983) *Readings on Language, Schools and Classrooms*. London: Methuen. *13, 149*

Stubbs, M., Robinson, B. and Twite, S. (1979) *Observing Classroom Language*. Block 5, PE232. Milton Keynes: Open University Press. *111*

Sutcliffe, D. (1981) *British Black English*. Oxford: Blackwell. *12, 68, 80*

Torode, B. (1976) Teacher's talk and classroom discipline. In Stubbs and Delamont (eds). *115, 135*

Tough, J. (1977) *The Development of Meaning*. London: Allen & Unwin. *79*

Trudgill, P. (1974) *Sociolinguistics*. Harmondsworth: Penguin. *29*

Trudgill, P. (1975a) *Accent, Dialect and the School*. London: Edward Arnold. *30, 34, 64, 150*

Trudgill, P. (1975b) Review of B. Bernstein *Class, Codes and Control*, vol 1. *Journal of Linguistics 11*, 1. *62, 65*

Trudgill, P. and Hannah, J. (1982) *International English: a Guide to Varieties of Standard English*. London: Edward Arnold. *37*

Turner, G. J. (1973) Social class and children's language of control at age 5 and age 7. In Bernstein (ed.) vol. 2. *54*

Walker, R. and Adelman, C. (1975a) *A Guide to Classroom Observation*. London: Methuen. *111–13, 143*

Walker, R. and Adelman, C. (1975b) Interaction analysis in informal classrooms: a critical comment on the Flanders system. *British Journal of Educational Psychology 45*, 1. *92, 111*

Walker, R. and Adelman, C. (1976) Strawberries. In Stubbs and Delamont (eds). *111–12*

Wells, G. *et al.* (1981) *Learning through Interaction*: vol. 1, *Language at Home and at School*. Cambridge: Cambridge University Press. *124*

Wells, J. C. (1982) *Accents of English*. 3 vols. Cambridge: Cambridge University Press. *12*

Wight, J. (1971) Dialect in school. *Educational Review 24*, I. *80*

Wight, J. (1975) Language through the looking glass. *Ideas*, Curriculum Magazine, Goldsmiths College, London, 31. *52, 80–1, 116*

Wight, J. (1979) Appendix: dialect and reading. In *Supplementary Readings for Block 4*, PE232. Milton Keynes: Open University Press. *83*

Wight, J. and Norris, R. (1970) *Teaching English to West Indian Children*, Schools Council Working Paper 29. London: Methuen. *80*

Wilkinson, A. (1971) *The Foundations of Language*. Oxford: Oxford University Press. *85*

Willes, M. (in press) *Children into Pupils: a Study of Language in Early Schooling*. London: Routledge & Kegan Paul. *13, 111, 115, 144, 150*

Young, M. F. D. (ed.) (1971) *Knowledge and Control*. London: Collier-Macmillan. *119, 121*